PARENT LIKE A PRO

The One-Stop-Shop Playbook of Tips, Strategies, and Real-Life Episodes

Brenda Reed Pilcher

foreword by: Bishop Henry M. Williamson, Sr.

Nonfiction Narrative

Handwritten inscription: Jamie, Thank amazing PARENT LIKE A PRO! Much Love, Brenda Reed Pilcher SGAC of Delta Sigma Theta 8/13/24 BRP

Disclaimer

The information and advice contained in this book are based upon the research and the personal and professional experiences of the author. They are not intended as a substitute for consulting with a professional. The publisher and author are not responsible for any adverse effects or consequences resulting from the use of any of the suggestions, preparations, or procedures discussed in this book.

Editor & Typesetter: Writluxe Writing Firm

Cover Designer: Takara M. Carter, Writluxe Writing Firm

First Photo: Tiny Tots Studio

Second photo: Wayne Franklin Photography

Manufactured in the United States of America

Library of Congress Control Number : 2022901251

E-book ISBN: 979-8-9855032-1-0

Print ISBN: 979-8-9855032-0-3

Printed in the United States of America

10 9 8 7 6 5 4 3 2 1

CONTENTS

I dedicate this book to the Holy Spirit, who guides me as a parent of our two exceptional gifts – Attorney Kelsi J. Pilcher and Teacher/Coach Henry Frank Pilcher, IV. Additionally, I dedicate my first book to the love of my life, Henry Frank Pilcher, III. Thank you for your unwavering love and support in my pursuit of becoming my best self.

FOREWORD

Parenting a child is one of the most difficult and challenging roles anyone can take on in life. Yet it is also one of the most rewarding roles an individual can have to be a mother, father, and caring adult!

Parent Like a Pro is an easy to read and informative book filled with lots of tips and strategies that can be used and followed by anyone wanting to be a better or great parent. It offers self-assessments to help you determine your parenting skills and style, all while letting you (or any parent) know adjustments can be made at any time to improve these skills.

As a parent and grandparent, I know the challenges one can face while raising children. And sometimes it is not easy to make the best decisions that will have a positive lasting effect on their lives. This book points out that LOVE is the one critical asset that can always aid you in making the best choices when parenting your children and/or grandchildren or foster children.

Bishop Henry M. Williamson, Sr. Presiding
Prelate, First Episcopal District Christian
Methodist Episcopal Church

PREFACE

I birthed this parenting book as a one-stop-shop for sharing parenting success tactics that I have learned as a parent educator for over three decades. I will also share some missteps along with successes on my journey as a parent of two awesome young adults – Attorney Kelsi Pilcher and Teacher/Coach Henry Pilcher IV.

One thing I know for sure is that love is not enough; good parenting requires information, strategies, skills, passion, patience, practice, purpose, and prayer. All of these elements combined are the essence of parenting like a pro, and not necessarily in that order. This is the parenting playbook I wish I had starting out as a first-time parent.

Since my faith is the cornerstone of my life, don't be surprised to see a few of my favorite scriptures in the book. These scriptures are not so much for parents themselves but rather for parents to guide their children.

The chapter titles are a conversion of seminar topics that I have researched and presented for over 30 years. Be EMPOWERED!

x

The Pilcher Family - 1995

The Pilcher Family Vacation - Sapphire Valley

CHAPTER ONE

Parenting with Positive Power

Outcomes

In this chapter, the parent/reader will discover the value of parenting with positive power. The focus is designed to help make the home a place where positive attitudes, self-worth, and success can be built.

> *"The greatest legacy one can pass on to one's children, and grandchildren is not money or other material things accumulated in one's life, but rather a legacy of character and faith."*
>
> BILLY GRAHAM – EVANGELIST

> *"Your words as a parent have great power. Use them wisely and make sure they come from the heart."*
>
> CAROLINA KING - AUTHOR

As parents, we know we are our children's first teachers. As we live our daily lives, we are writing a parenting playbook where our children will follow our directions and model our behaviors. Let's be careful as parents what we write in our parenting playbook and be ever mindful of our illustrations. The parenting playbook that we write for our children will influence their decisions for the rest of their lives. It is never too late to edit the legacy we will leave for our children, their children, and many generations to come.

My goal for chapter one is to help the parent/reader

become intentional about leaving a legacy that will strengthen their families and their entire communities.

The best way to start making your home a place where positive attitudes, self-worth, and success can be built is to get to know your child. Your child's personality was being formed in the womb. Some fetuses kick and move, while others are calm and seldom kick or move about. We have all heard that our unborn children can sense our emotions. Whether we are happy or sad, they know it and are affected by that emotion.

Hence, babies are born with personalities, but the environment in which they are born and nurtured will make the most significant impact on who they ultimately become.

Parenting with Positive Power requires skillful thinking and planning. We can all learn to do this better, and here are a few things to consider.

Physical needs: This means doing all we can to help our children grow up healthy and safe. Remember, children learn habits by watching us. Whether these habits are good or bad, they will do more of what they see us do.

Eating healthy is a habit that can last for a lifetime. I enjoyed taking my children to the grocery store. We would discuss what was good for your health and what was not. They always wanted to weigh the produce on the scale in the produce section. I taught them that the healthier choices were not down the aisles, but rather outside the corridors, like meats, fruits, and vegetables.

My mantra was, if you don't buy a lot of junk food, they won't eat a lot of junk food.

We encouraged our children to ask questions. When I said "no" to something that they wanted, I took the time to explain why. A case and point is when our daughter wanted a soda versus water, I would describe the health and beauty benefits of drinking more water. It usually worked. When our son wanted an unhealthy snack, I would explain the choices that would help him build muscle mass. Explaining why and why not regarding something they cared about or wanted made things a bit easier. My goal was to teach them to make healthy choices, even when I wasn't around. It's not just a cliché; knowledge is power!

Being active in physical activities is a family affair. Exposure is the key to helping your children find their niche. Something as simple as a family walk around the neighborhood or in the park can be fun and educational. Even if the children are in a stroller or a wagon, spend time outside every day. When we help our children fall in love with nature, it adds a whole new dimension to how they see the world.

Additionally, as parents, we are responsible for attending to the **emotional needs** of our children. We must show love, attention, and give encouragement. This will help them build self-worth and form healthy relationships within the family and with others. When we spend time with our children engaging in activities that they love, this shows them how much we care for them. In my case, our children had input into how we should spend our family time together. They were raised to respectfully have and articulate their opinions.

My parents raised me in a loving and affectionate environment, which made it easy for me to do the same for my family. This should make you ask yourself, do you hug your children every day? How do you want to be remembered, "warm and affectionate" or "cold and distant?"

Aforementioned, powerful parenting requires more than just LOVE, but LOVE is the starting point. The truth of the matter is, LOVE will set everything else in motion. Find ways to let your children know how much you love them every day.

This starts at birth – cuddling, singing, and yes reading are just a few ways we can show love. As children grow older, spend time listening and talking to them and staying involved in what they like to do. "I love you" are the three most important words we can say to our children every day.

We can easily overlook the emotional needs of our children when we spend a lot of time with them. Just spending time is not enough. It's important for us to stay connected with them and ask our children, "How are you doing?"

As your children grow, so does your role as a parent. In addition to their emotional and physical needs, children also have **intellectual needs.** This is the innate need to learn and master new skills. Allowing your toddler to pick up and eat one cheerio at a time teaches eye-hand coordination. Of course, you could feed it to him, but why not allow this critical motor skill to flourish. Praise will go a long way as they learn and master new skills.

I will never forget when our daughter decided that T-Ball would be her first sport. When we arrived at the first practice, little did we know that she would be the only girl. I was so disappointed, but not Kelsi. She decided that she would not only stay for the practice but also finish out the season. Not surprising, she won the most improved player award at the end-of-season awards picnic. We have always encouraged her to "just try." She learned early that she could master many things if she would only work for it.

At age four, our son decided he would try soccer as his first sport. Remember our mantra, "just try." Well, Henry Frank "just tried" and was one of the best and fastest on the team. Kicking the soccer ball in mid-air, the crowd, mostly parents, would cheer him on. He stuck with it until his dad introduced him to his favorite sport, Football! Although he wanted to play both, he had to make a decision. His school work was a top priority, so one sport was all we could manage... or all that I could manage.

At the time, I was a full-time education consultant working with teachers and parents alike. I would frequently advise parents not to over-schedule their children with too many activities. I would add, "Try to spend as much time with them as you can, because when your children spend all of their time with others, those "others" become a significant influence. Pay attention to who those "others" are and make sure those "others" share your value system."

Include stories about yourself when talking with your children. Our children enjoyed hearing about our childhood. We would talk and laugh, all while strengthening our family bond. We were intentional about what we poured into our children. Praise is another thing that every child needs, but our praise must be authentic.

Children can quickly become immune to hearing the same praise words over and over. Rather than saying "good job", be specific. Give examples like: "I like how you stay within the lines when you color your picture." Or, "Thank you for saying yes ma'am and yes sir during our family discussions." When I asked my son how the spelling test went that I helped him study the night before, "I aced it" was his reply! I then praised him by saying, "Nice work! Studying for that test really paid off!"

Children feel loved when you make eye contact with them while they are talking. It's essential that you really listen and allow them to finish before you speak. When you take the time to ask questions, it shows that you were listening. This is not the easiest thing to do when you are multi-tasking, but it is vital.

Teach your children that they can be open and honest with you about their thoughts and feelings. This is an excellent way to get to know your children individually

and collectively. Praise them for making the right decisions, and don't hesitate to be specific. Remember, this is
all about building a relationship of love, trust, and mutual
respect. The more secure they feel at home, the more
successful they will feel outside of the home.

Allow your children to make mistakes. Sometimes
when we know that our children will not be successful, we
have a tendency to want to help them. Children are no
different from us. They learn more from their mistakes.
We can help them to feel good about their successes and
accept and learn from their failures. Someone once said,
"you only fail when you stop trying."

It's important to remember that our children need
roots and wings. Ensure that they are grounded with
strong morals and values, then set them on a path to try
out their wings until they are ready to fly solo.

It's easy to forget that one of the most essential
parenting skills is managing ourselves. Knowing our
parenting style and what we know to be true about our
beliefs and actions will allow us to be intentional about
the parenting playbook we are writing. It's imperative not
just to make an impact, but we must make an impact that
will last throughout their lives. It's all about building a
legacy. Decide what you want your legacy to be and take
steps that are intentional, one day at a time. We all have
actions and beliefs that can be tweaked for a better
outcome.

What's Your Parenting Style?: Used by Permission:
Active Parenting Publishers

Take this quiz to find out! It is divided into two parts with
15 statements each. Part I is designed to help you identify
your beliefs about being a parent. Part II focuses on your
current home situation. As you read each statement,
decide how much you agree with it. Then write the
number from 1 to 5 that corresponds to your level of
agreement: 1. strongly disagree; 2. disagree; 3. neutral; 4.
agree; 5. strongly agree

Part I: Beliefs

1. It is better to give a little ground and protect
   the peace than to stand firm and provoke a
   fight. 1 2 3 4 5
2. Children need discipline that hurts a little so
   that they will remember the lesson later. 1 2 3
   4 5
3. Children shouldn't always get their way, but
   usually we ought to learn to listen to what they
   have to say. 1 2 3 4 5
4. The parent-child relationship is like a war in
   which if the parent wins, both sides win; but if
   the parent loses, both sides lose. 1 2 3 4 5
5. If parents provide a good environment,

children will pretty much raise themselves. 1 2
3 4 5

6. 6. The parent's role is like that of a teacher
who is preparing the child for a final exam
called life. 1 2 3 4 5

7. Childhood is so short that parents should do
everything to make it a happy time. 1 2 3 4 5

8. "Spare the rod and spoil the child" is still the
best policy. 1 2 3 4 5

9. Children need to learn what they may or may
not do, but we don't have to use punishment to
teach. 1 2 3 4 5

10. Whether we like it or not, children have the
last word about what they will or won't do. 1 2
3 4 5

11. If you let children have pretty free rein, they
will eventually learn from the consequences of
their behavior what is appropriate. 1 2 3 4 5

12. Children first have to learn that the parent is
boss. 1 2 3 4 5

13. Too many children today talk back to their
parents when they should just quietly obey
them. 1 2 3 4 5

14. If we want children to respect us, we must first
treat them with respect. 1 2 3 4 5

15. You can never do too much for your child if it
comes from genuine love. 1 2 3 4 5

Part II: Actions

1. I often have to call my child more than once to get her or him out of bed in the morning. 1 2 3 4 5

2. I have to constantly stay on top of my child to get things done. 1 2 3 4 5

3. When my child misbehaves, he or she usually knows what the consequences will be. 1 2 3 4 5

4. I often get angry and yell at my child. 1 2 3 4 5

5. I often feel that my child is taking advantage of my good nature. 1 2 3 4 5

6. We have discussed chores at our home and everybody takes part. 1 2 3 4 5

7. My child gets a spanking at least once a month. 1 2 3 4 5

8. My child has no regular chores around the home, but will occasionally pitch in when asked. 1 2 3 4 5

9. I usually give my child clear instructions as to how I want something done. 1 2 3 4 5

10. My child is a finicky eater, so I have to try various combinations to make sure he or she gets the proper nutrition. 1 2 3 4 5

11. I don't call my child names, and I don't expect to be called names by my child. 1 2 3 4 5

12. I usually give my child choices between two

appropriate alternatives rather than telling my child what to do. 1 2 3 4 5

13. I have to threaten my child with punishment at least once a week. 1 2 3 4 5

14. I wish my child wouldn't interrupt my conversations so often. 1 2 3 4 5

15. My child usually gets up and ready without my help in the morning. 1 2 3 4 5

Scoring your questionnaire: To determine your style as a parent, first transfer your score for each item to the blanks beside the following item numbers listed in parentheses. (Put your score for item #2 in the first blank, item #4 in the second blank, and so on.) Then add your scores in each row across, and put the sum in the last blank. Autocratic belief score: (2) _____ + (4) _____ + (8) _____ + (12) _____ + (13) _____ = _____ Permissive belief score: (1) _____ + (5) _____ + (7) _____ + (11) _____ + (15) _____ = _____ Active* belief score: (3) _____ + (6) _____ + (9) _____ + (10) _____ + (14) _____ = _____ Autocratic action score: (17) _____ + (19) _____ + (22) _____ + (24) _____ + (28) _____ = _____ Permissive action score: (16) _____ + (20) _____ + (23) _____ + (25) _____ + (29) _____ = _____ Active* action score: (18) _____ + (21) _____ + (26) _____ + (27) _____ + (30) _____ = _____

To get a clearer look at how your scores on the three styles compare, transfer each of the six totals to the appropriate blank in the table below. To get your combined scores, add your belief score and your action score for each of the three styles. Put these numbers in the blanks in the "Combined" column.

Belief + Action = Combined

Autocratic _____ + _____ = _____

Permissive _____ + _____ = _____

Active* _____ + _____ = _____

Interpreting your scores: The highest combined score possible for each style is 50. The higher your score, the more you tend toward that style of parenting. Your highest combined score, therefore, suggests the style of parenting you are currently using. If either of the other combined scores is within fifteen points of your highest score, consider your use of the two styles about equal. The greater the difference among scores, the greater your current preference for the style with the highest score. Differences of more than fifteen points between belief scores and action scores for any style suggest that you tend to believe one thing, but do another. Do not be alarmed by this. It is common and understandable. **High Autocratic Score** - If you're like most people, you'll find yourself more autocratic than you thought you were. But after all, this was the predominant style parents used when you were growing up.

---

* The Active style is sometimes called the "Authoritative" or "Democratic" style.

. . .

If you scored highest on this style, you probably find yourself in frequent battles with your child. Anger and frustration probably characterize the power struggles that you and your child experience. You are probably reading this web page to find some relief, as well as a more successful approach. **High Permissive Score** - In an attempt to avoid being autocratic, you may have over-compensated and developed a permissive style. If you are in this group, your relationship with your child may be pretty good as long as you do what your child wants. But you probably find that your child gets very hostile, and perhaps even throws tantrums, when you do say no or make a demand of him or her. Your relationship is characterized by service and pleasing, but only in one direction. You may have already begun to resent this unfairness. If so, you probably scored higher on the autocratic scale than you expected. It is easy to get fed up with a permissive approach and flip back to an autocratic one. **High Active Score** - If you scored highest on the active style, your relationship with your child is probably already positive. Though problems certainly occur, an atmosphere of mutual respect, trust, and teamwork enables you to handle them without the hurt or resentment that characterize the other styles. You are probably using many of the methods advocated and taught in Active Parenting courses at this website. Our goal is to support your efforts and help you discover other compatible techniques.

Permission granted to reprint this Parenting Quiz for use in parenting groups. Reprints must include Active Parenting's name and contact information (800-825-0060 and www.ActiveParenting.com). Books and other resources that teach Active Parenting.

Consider your responses to the Parenting Quiz.

What is your parenting style?
Are you happy with your answers?
In which areas do you need improvement?

Choose one or two areas to celebrate.
Choose one or two areas to improve.

As I bring chapter one to a close...Here is a prayer to be prayed over your children often.

Create in our children a pure heart O God, and renew
in them a right spirit.
Psalm 51:10 KJV

Adapted by the Author

Chapter Two

How to Raise Critical Thinkers

Outcomes

In this chapter, the parent/reader will unveil strategies to model and promote six critical thinking skills at home.

> *"The whole world opened up to me when I learned to read."*
> Mary McCleod Bethune - American Educator and Civil Rights Activist

> *"Reading without reflecting is like eating without digesting."*
> Edmund Burke - Philosopher

What does it mean to think critically? According to the Oxford dictionary, critical thinking allows the thinker to skillfully analyze and assess a subject, content, or problem at varying levels. We will explore these different levels of thinking critically, but first, let's explore why it is essential to promote it at home.

Critical thinking allows the thinker to think rationally and clearly about what to do or believe in a given situation. It is synonymous with being an independent thinker who understands the logical connection between ideas. As an educator, I know first-hand that critical thinking skills are the most vital skills for success at home, school, and life.

There is a hierarchy when it comes to promoting six

critical thinking skills at home. The key is to make it fun. Demonstrate the fun your children will have by:

- Becoming a Detective: To encourage observing and questionings skills
- Becoming a Builder: To promote classifying and sorting
- Becoming a Teacher: To develop compare and contrast
- Becoming a Researcher: To help with summarizing
- Becoming a Scientist: To promote hypothesizing
- Becoming an Attorney: To encourage decision making

Emphasizing these skills should start at a very early age, and here are some ways that parents can model and promote thinking critically at home.

Remembering that every child is unique and will learn these critical skills at different rates with varying depth of knowledge is paramount.

The first critical thinking skill is to teach your child to be a detective through observing and questioning. Becoming an excellent critical thinker will depend on these two things. Teaching your child to be a detective can be fun, especially during those walks outside. By pointing out what you see along the way can lend itself to great learning experiences—things like squirrels, butterflies, bugs, birds, and my son's favorite caterpillars.

Yes, the caterpillar became an obsession for him, which taught us all more caterpillar facts than most people know about their dogs. It was a while before I realized that he was collecting them and transporting them in his pocket and breeding moths in a shoebox in his bedroom. He learned that caterpillars were herbivorous, so he filled the shoebox with grass. According to his calculation, it took about three weeks before the caterpillar metamorphosized into a moth.

Once they became moths, he was satisfied to set them free, and sometimes there were up to 10 in his box. He would then start the breeding process all over again.

Once you get your children hooked on observing, ask questions to get them to think deeper. Questions like... what purpose do they serve? Why do you think they behave a certain way?

The Ant Farm became his next point of interest. The funny thing is, whatever he took an interest in, we all took part in it. Through the eyes of your children, you can learn so much. These experiences can also teach them to appreciate small things. Watching ants on the ant farm can be incredible to observe. It was like watching people in a busy city. There is a non-stop movement, and if you watched them long enough, you could detect just how social they are. They stop and interact with each other just like we do. Ants are also builders and carry food and supplies needed to set up shop. They appear to be very content with their existence.

When children spend time outside, there is much to observe. Through these observations, many questions will arise, and the more they question, the more they learn.

As a reading advocate, I would always try to tie a book to whatever the kids were interested in. Allowing your kids to teach you facts about what they are interested in only leads to more observations and more questions. I still remember a few fun facts that I learned from my very young son at the time:

- There are about a million ants to every single human being.
- There are many different species of ants.
- Queen Ant can live up to 30 years.
- Our species of ants were called the Runner Ant because of their fast movement.

Learning about nature is fun and entertaining but doesn't discount the opportunity to promote critical thinkers inside your home. When reading together, I would ask my children, "How did this story make you feel?" I always followed up with "why?" Why questions require more thinking. I attempted to ask questions that required some thought. I call these open-ended questions because they cannot be answered with "yes" or "no." Case in point: instead of asking your child, "How was school today?" which will usually resort to the infamous reply,

"Fine," ask your child, "What did he learn today in science?" Always start with their favorite subject. They are more likely to engage in a conversation about science. Another frequent question I asked was, "What was the most fun you had today?" If you helped your child study spelling words the night before, always inquire, "How did it go?"

Another great way to encourage critical thinking through observing and questioning is a good old fashion scavenger hunt. This can take many forms, whether you are indoors or out. Examples: Look around the house and find everything with a rectangle shape. When the kids were small, we would confine their search to one room. Ask why these objects were shaped a certain way? Why is the shape relevant to its purpose? Beware, "why" questions take a bit more time to formulate answers. Your patience will pay off with tremendous rewards. What about things in their closet with different textures for different seasons and color palettes? Ask how many things they can find that are taller, same, or shorter than they are?

Our favorite outside scavenger hunt was to lay down face up on a blanket or the trampoline and find clouds with animal shapes. This can become interesting as clouds do move, especially on a sunny day. For our children, cloud watching sparked an interest in photography. Their interest in sky colors and cloud formations became a massive hobby.

Their sky photo collection became a big topic of

conversation over dinner and had to be displayed and shared with all visitors. It's helpful when others encourage your children. Family, friends, teachers, pastors, and neighbors can significantly impact your child's learning and self-esteem.

Another fun indoor activity that we enjoyed that enhanced their observing and questioning skills was observing while I prepared a meal. They had to write down the order of things from start to finish. When we reviewed their notes, it led to more questions and even more laughter.

The next time we spent time in the kitchen together, they each had to prepare a snack consisting of at least four ingredients. First, they had to write down the steps, then follow those steps to make their snack. Hint... they were not allowed to veer off from their notes. This will require them to think critically during the planning stage. Again, this led to more questions and even more laughter. As you can see, there are so many ways to make learning to think critically fun.

Let's move on to another aspect of critical thinking. This will require you to teach your child to become a builder. It's called classifying or sorting. I will share examples of how this can be accomplished practically and painlessly. First, I want you to think of classifying in this way...

classifying is arranging or sorting a group of people, things, classes, and categories according to shared qualities or characteristics. An excellent place to start is by assigning a word for each alphabet from A – Z.

For even younger children, the abacus has stood the test of time for teaching so many skills. Classifying or sorting is just one of the many. Building blocks is another long-standing manipulative used in our home. You can focus on color, size, shape, counting, and more as you sort or classify. When focusing on size, ask which is big, bigger, and biggest? There may only be a slight difference in the size, so ask your child to demonstrate the differences.

Food for Thought

Through everyday conversations, parents can help their children become better communicators and critical thinkers by doing more asking than telling.

Admittedly, critical thinking is a complex skill that goes beyond the mundane or typical thought pattern. This is why it's crucial and will set your children up for more success at home, school, and life.

As a family, we enjoyed sorting and classifying. It especially came in handy when I wanted help to set the table for dinner. The kids would divide the tasks and choose which plates, cups, spoons, forks, and knives to use. They enjoyed sorting our diverse selection of glassware. I would ask them why were the glasses, different shapes and sizes? What is their purpose? They quickly learned the difference between casual dishes and those meant for more formal affairs.

Saying we are the "Pilchers" was repeated often in our home. I taught the kids to say this to emphasize that we don't always follow what society deems as normal. Because of my extensive background working with parents and listening to what works and, more importantly, what does not work, I had a good handle on what would be acceptable for the "Pilchers."

You will understand the importance of establishing who you are as a family, as I will reference many times throughout the chapters.

Classification helped our children make sense of the world around them. This was especially true when it came to animals. It all started with our trips to the zoo. Before they were readers, Henry and I would read aloud all the information for each animal. They would place the animals in various categories and knew early that the tiger was a mammal, a warm-blooded animal, and a carnivore makes the tiger a meat-eater.

They later created their category charts with more details. Not surprisingly, this led to more reading about animals.

To this day, the library holds unforgettable memories for us as a family. Kelsi and Henry Frank both had library cards before they were able to sign their names in cursive.

Their reading interest was limitless. Reading books

about animals, books about plants, books about insects, you name it, they read it.

Before long, they debated where various plants, animals, and even insects originated and the environment in which they thrive.

It was insatiable how learning led to more knowledge. Soon we were discussing geography. These discussions would far exceed the United States. It was clear that someone would be getting a globe for Christmas. Soon they were able to point out where Polar Bears and elephants originated. They had a tremendous sense of space and the world around them. Our family discussions often involved a considerable number of questions and answers.

Even today, our young adults are never satisfied with just the answer; they want to know "why."

Once becoming a detective – observing and questioning and a builder – classifying and sorting have been set in motion, it's time to put on the teacher's hat. Becoming a teacher was their favorite. Children love exchanging roles with those in charge, like parents and teachers. This is where the critical thinking skills compare and contrast come into play. Encourage your children to become and think like a teacher.

When it was time to plan a vacation, we would compare our options. For instance, a beach vacation would expose our kids to water sports and allow them to put their years of swim lessons into action. The beach vacation was generally more cost-effective once we arrived. Packing a picnic for a day at the beach ensured money was left over for souvenirs.

Another option to consider was a city vacation. Having more of a cultural experience with live performances, museums, and parks framed a robust conversation around the dinner table. Having these discussions as a family, modeled compare and contrast for the kids in real-time. These discussions often resulted in debates. As they were learning how to compare and contrast, Henry and I observed who our kids would later become...Kelsi the Attorney and Henry Frank the High School History Teacher and Football Coach.

Another way to think of compare and contrast is to look at the similarities and differences.

When reading or watching a family movie, compare and contrast can take on a different meaning. Ask your children to compare their favorite character with that of another. How do they contrast or differ? Children can become introspective when you ask them to compare or contrast themselves with a character in a movie, book, or comic strip.

Admittedly, as a former classroom teacher, many of my questioning techniques came naturally. I had to put forth a real effort not to sound "teacherfied." After our kids spent all day at school with their teachers, the last thing they needed was to come home to another one. My role as a mother, especially after a long day at school, was to become more of a facilitator. I would allow the children to guide the conversation while gathering the information I needed regarding their school day, teachers, and friends.

Showing an interest in your child's friends will help them to make better choices.

The next step in modeling critical thinking skills at home is to allow your children to become researchers. The power of summarizing will undoubtedly be one of the most important critical thinking skills, and this is why.

Let's start with what is summarizing. To summarize something means to take something long and shorten it, while highlighting what's most important.

When I told the kids that being able to summarize makes them a researcher, they embraced it.

To summarize text, conversation, or pictures, you must first totally understand it.

As a classroom teacher and education consultant, I taught children and adults the art of "close reading." It is also a reading strategy for teaching summarizing in reading comprehension. Simply put, it means reading something closely, allowing you to recall or summarize details when needed.

This example resonated with our children big time. On the first day of school, when the teacher summons you to share verbally or in writing, "what did you do over the summer?" You don't give her a day-to-day account, but rather the highlights or essential stuff. Your vacation destination or getting a new puppy is a summary.

When the kids matriculated to reading chapter books, I gave them a set of index cards (colorful, of course) to summarize each chapter. When they returned to school to take an AR (Accelerated Reader) quiz, they would study their card summaries and earn high comprehension scores via the computer.

Summarizing encapsulates other comprehension skills like main idea, sequencing, recall details, context clues, and more. It is a critical thinking skill that is used in every subject.

For those of you who thought this might be difficult, I hope you can breathe a sigh of relief at how painless and practical this process can be.

Teaching your children to think critically will require patience. Here are a few critical responses to try...

Turn-ons
"Good question."
"You were pretty smart to think of that."
"That's an interesting way to look at it."
"I like the way you think."

Turn-offs
"Don't ask so many questions."
"You are too young to ask a question."
"I don't have time right now."
"Children are to be seen and not heard."

. . .

Every child has a scientist hidden inside. When you predict the outcome of something based on what you already know or have learned, you form a hypothesis. I like thinking of this as making an educated guess. Encouraging this critical thinking skill can be fun for the whole family.

Think about this. Predicting the outcome of a football game or tennis match could create excitement in the home. The more you know about the team, or better yet, the players, the better your hypothesis. What about predicting the outcome of a story?

This could become a game that could elicit some robust conversations about political elections, the gender of an unborn child, weather, or even report cards.

Remember those grocery store trips where the kids would weigh the produce? Making a hypothesis regarding the weight of produce added another layer to grocery shopping. The one with the most accurate prediction or explanation earned a treat.

After a while, they became so astute at predicting the weight of produce we had to move on to a more challenging hypothesis.

As a family of readers, we would search the newspaper for current events and follow certain headlines to determine the most accurate hypothesis. Be creative. Once the kids get the hang of it, they will have many suggestions to keep it entertaining.

Finally, the highest level of critical thinking is an evaluation or making a judgment/decision.

According to the Cambridge Dictionary, evaluation is the process of judging or calculating the quality, importance, amount, or value of something. There are countless ways to emphasize and model this significant acquisition at home. It's a great way to encourage your child to look at all sides of an issue.

We don't often think of this as evaluation, but when our children decide who they will befriend is a judgment or evaluation. It's anything that requires weighing pros and cons. Encourage your children to share their decisions with you with emphasis on the "why."

Sharing stories with your family that involve a decision that you had to make will help put them at ease during these conversations. Perhaps you were offered a promotion at work, and you had to decide if more money was worth leaving a position and a supportive team that you loved.

As your children become older, their evaluations and decision-making will become more complex. Helping them to weigh the pros and cons early on will ensure good decision-makers later in life.

We always taught the kids to never make a rash decision about essential matters. Then we would advise them to pray about it, sleep on it, then trust your judgment.

Another strategy that we used with the kids was to write it down. On a piece of paper with a line drawn down the middle, write pros on one side and cons on the other. Creating this visual allowed the kids to see that evaluation is not always cut and dry. Sometimes there is more than one right answer or judgment.

I hope I have demonstrated how teaching this complex skill of critical thinking can be fun and rewarding for the whole family.

This age-old adage still holds true...to stimulate critical thinking, ask questions that begin with "who," "what," "when," "where," "why," and "how."

God bless our children to always pray and not faint, lose heart, or give up.

Luke 18:1 KJV

Adapted by the Author

CHAPTER THREE

Parents as Homework Advocates:
Raising the Bar for our Children

Outcomes

In this chapter, the parent/reader will discover ways to help their children tackle homework with ease while learning the importance of becoming a homework advocate.

> *"Children are likely to live up to what you believe of them."*
> Lady Bird Johnson – Former First Lady of the United States

> *"You can learn many things from children. How much patience you have, for instance."*
> Franklin P. Jones – American Humorist

Parenting is an action verb. Without our active engagement, how will our children successfully manage: family time, studying, tests, assignments, projects, extra-curricular activities, church, and friends. Our kids have so many things to juggle as they navigate the learning expectations of school, home, and life. To help them do this successfully, I want to share some strategies that worked for me as a parent and some I learned from parents and grandparents during my life as a parent advocate and educator.

These are a few must-haves for learning at home; pens, pencils, crayons, scissors, paper, planner, physical and electronic books, and a dictionary. You will discover that learning doesn't require a lot of supplies. What it does need is something that money can't buy, focus and motivation.

In fact, household items can easily be used to keep our children engaged. After all, learning begins at home.

Let's start with the organization.

Like most things, the younger you start teaching your child organizational skills, the better. For us, this meant teaching toddlers to put toys away after playtime. Kelsi learned the craft of same and different by lining up her shoes on her closet floor. After they were organized in pairs, she would count them.

Children are no different from parents when it comes to organization. When our living and workspaces are well-organized, we accomplish so much more.

For our children, this meant identifying an area of our home for school work. All of the school supplies I have listed should be easily accessible in that location.

Our school supplies were stored in 2 separate baskets and tucked under their beds until it was time for learning.

Being a working mom, I mastered multitasking to accomplish more. During the kid's early years, the kitchen table was homework central while I prepared dinner. The kids would routinely settle in at the dinner table with their basket of supplies and a light snack as I prepare dinner.

Being in close proximity to them during homework, I

was agile enough to stop and attend to their questions. They learned self-efficacy by utilizing our home resources like the dictionary, calculator, or each other before I stepped in to help. I mastered the art of stirring up a pot with one hand while holding a list of spelling words in the other.

By my calculation, if homework was completed by the time I finished dinner, we could all eat dinner together and discuss our day. Our kids were just as interested in how Henry and I spent our day as we were in theirs.

Those neighborhood walks and sometimes to the nearby park were a daily occurrence, weather permitting. The sheer enjoyment of our daily walks was the focus and motivation the kids needed to complete assignments just in time for dinner.

As the kids grew older and their assignments became more demanding, I introduced the daily planner. It helped us keep track of daily tasks, future projects, study time, test dates, and any practices or rehearsals.

Kelsi being the eldest, mastered the skill of organization and using the daily planner first. Not only did she enjoy listing her many assignments and tasks in her planner, she would also allow Henry Frank to dictate what to write in his.

He enjoyed her being in charge up until age three. At this point, he decided she was not his boss and would remind her often.

When we observed self-efficacy taking hold, we invested in a desk and chair for each of their rooms. It was something about having their desk and chair in their private space that made studying and reading even more satisfying.

Now that they were out of the kitchen doing their homework, I had to modify my routine.

They continued to solicit my help after exhausting their other resources. My new role consisted of checking the planner against the actual assignment.

To this day, Kelsi enjoys keeping a list of things to do. Henry Frank has always marched to the beat of his own drum. Recently, he shared with me that he keeps a daily planner. I whispered a prayer of thankfulness.

What I know for sure...when you make learning enjoyable, kids will engage in the learning.

Most homes are equipped with some of the following supplies. Activities created using these household items can be as simple or as complex as needed for age appropriateness.

Newspaper, sales, grocery ads, sports ads
Playing cards
Canned food labels and food packages
Clock or timer
Ruler, measuring tape, or yardstick
Cash register receipts
Coupons
Calendars
Egg cartons

Money - coins or bills

Magazines

Pencil and paper

Recipes

Cell phone

Laptop or PC

Books

Please share this list with your kids and ask them to create activities to incorporate these items. Then go beyond the basics, incorporate science, art, math, and language arts. There is no limit when creative minds meet.

Before starting with things your child struggles with, choose an activity using household items they will master.

As a classroom teacher, I witnessed first-hand that a motivated student was easier to teach. The same is true for your kids when learning at home. Whether it is home-work assigned by the teacher or me, the child must be motivated.

Try providing a myriad of learning opportunities to allow your children to develop their interests and build their skill capacity. Then once they establish what they are good at, use this opportunity to build confidence, motiva-tion, and reduce anxiety.

Self-confidence and motivation frequently come from extra-curricular activities.

Surprising myself, I became a pageant mom. Not like the ones you see on TV. When Kelsi was walking but still in diapers, I entered her in her first pageant. After winning several in a row and being rewarded with toys galore and trophies, she called it quits. OK, I called it quits. The awarding of cash and scholarships were not the norm 30 years ago. Her biggest win was

her being crowned Little Miss LaPetite in a state-wide competition. Kelsi reigned as the winner for Tennessee and then went to Tampa, Florida in pursuit of a national crown. She did not win the national crown, but she was recognized for her photo. She received an honorable mention for most photogenic. There were so many toddlers sad and screaming as if to say, Abuse! Abuse! Kelsi took it all in stride. She gazed at those who were disgruntled with such compassion.

It was our first vacation since her birth and her first visit to a beach. So, I called it a win-win and the end of pageants.

She then took up dancing. This time it was her idea. Like everything else she tried, she advanced to the top in tap, ballet, and jazz. Building confidence in these activities helped her gain assurance in academics.

Aforementioned, T-ball came next for Kelsi. I learned from observing other parents not to allow our ambitions to steal our kid's joy. Yes, I preferred that she dance over T-ball, but she was determined. After all, T-ball was a summer-only sport, so I conceded.

She continued to dance for several years and appeared to have enjoyed it. However, I learned later that it was the make-up and costumes that she loved and not necessarily the art of dance.

By the time Henry Frank arrived, I was a four-year mom with many life lessons under my belt. He accompanied Kelsi to piano lessons for summer camp, to my immense pleasure, he took to it and asked to take piano lessons as well. He was a little shy during the recitals but stuck with it for nine months, three weeks, and two days.

Being a somewhat seasoned mom, I realized that this was how children find their niche. Exposure. Here's the thing, exposure can be tricky because it does cost time and money. I had two goals in mind. First, find your niche, and second, finish what you start. In the case of Henry Frank and those piano lessons, I gave my three-year-old son a break.

At age four, he chose soccer as his first sport. It was evident he had found his niche. I spoke about his athletic ability in an earlier chapter. Soccer was Henry Frank's claim to fame from age four to 5th-grade. Building their interests and skills were realized through games, puzzles, and reading various genres of books.

Our family time was nothing short of amazing. Our mission as parents was to help them see the connection between effort, skill, and performance. We used encouraging phrases like, "don't give up", "you got this"," you can do it", and "your hard work is paying off."

I will also point out, try not to compare your child's performance with that of other children. What's important is their individual progress.

Knowing your children and recognizing their differences is paramount. How do they learn best? Through observation and helping with homework, you will be able to identify how your children learn best. Most children fall into one or more of these categories.

Visual Learners – learn best by seeing what they are learning. Using charts and graphs, maps, flashcards, and graphic organizers will help cement their learning.

Auditory Learners – learn best by hearing what they are learning. Using oral presentations, audiobooks, calling out math facts or rhymes will help cement their learning.

Kinesthetic Learners – learn best through movement. Using skits, plays, or standing while studying or reading will keep this learner alert and engaged in cementing their learning.

Most kids learn best by combining visual, auditory, and kinesthetics. Encourage all of these methods to find the best fit. Your children will let you know what makes them feel successful.

A homework advocate monitors homework assignments and provides immediate feedback. Set high expectations for neatness and organization. Be careful how you respond to failure. No one is perfect. Point out that more studying is required. Pay attention to what tests and assignments are due. Teach them that procrastination renders poor results. Emphasize that we study to learn, not just to pass a test or get a good grade. Sometimes I caught myself speaking to my kids the way I talked to my students. I would say we cement the learning by reviewing it over and over. It always resulted in them giving me the brick-and-mortar stare. Being intentional in the following areas can go a long way.

Here are strategies that worked for us:

- Get organized.
- Establish routines.
- Set Goals.
- Set aside time to study.
- Study even if you don't have homework.
- Read for pleasure.
- Talk about what you are reading.
- Practice self-efficacy.
- Seek tutoring if needed.
- Investigate what tutoring is available through the school first.

Is tutoring your child a good idea? There is no wrong or right answer; however, in my experience bringing in a third party was helpful. Sometimes when your child is struggling, you are the last person they want help from. Children inherently want to show their parents their best performance. We know that every child is different, so ask them their preference and don't take it personally.

How much help is too much help? As a homework advocate, it was my goal to teach independence and provide encouragement. As the kids grew older, I became more of a cheerleader and less of a homework helper. The beauty in starting at an early age is that your children will begin implementing the strategies listed above independently. Your role as a homework helper will evolve, but your commitment to being a homework advocate will always be a requisite.

Another aspect of being a homework advocate is to team up with your child's teachers. Let them know you are there to support them in educating your child. No one likes to admit this but, children receive more attention at school when the parents have a relationship with the teacher. Create an open line of communication with the teacher. Make sure they know your face and your name. Have a list of questions when attending parent-teacher conferences. Hold your child and his teacher accountable. It takes a village to raise a child is not a cliché. It is how we raise well-rounded children. You cannot do it alone and do it well.

Asking your child's teacher for help is one of the best ways to help your child. Know what the expectations are for your child and make sure they understand them. Spending time at your child's school is a great way to know if your child is getting the optimal learning experience.

Here are a few suggestions:

- Be a Parent Volunteer.
- Serve on the Parent Advisory Board.
- Join the PTA – Parent-Teacher Association.
- Attend parent-teacher conferences.

- Attend special school events.
- Attend open house.
- Visit book fairs.
- Attend live performances.

The number one question that I was asked by parents of children of all ages: What is the recommended time to spend on homework? My staple answer is what I learned during my undergraduate studies at the University of Arkansas at Pine Bluff.

Multiply the grade of your child times 10.

For example: a first grader should spend **at least** 10 minutes each evening reading or completing a homework assignment.

Third grade – 30 minutes

Sixth grade – 60 minutes

Eighth grade - 80 minutes

Eleventh grade – 110 minutes, etc.

Remember, you don't have to be an expert. Make homework a habit, and don't forget the hugs!

Lord bless our children to be responsible and bear their own burden.

Galatians 6:5 KJV

Adapted by the Author

Chapter Four

Parents Helping Children Develop a Love for Reading

Outcomes

In this chapter, the parent/reader will learn simple tips for teaching reading at home using strategies to lead to a love for reading.

"Once you learn to read, you will be forever free."
Frederick Douglass - American Abolitionist, Orator and Writer

Reading is to the mind what exercise is to the body.
Joseph Addison - English Essayist, Playwright and Poet

Repeat after me... I am my child's first teacher. My home is my child's first school. Reading is my child's first subject. For three decades, this was how I opened every parent seminar. For some parents, this may go without saying, but for others, not so much. It was not unusual to hear parents murmuring: I can't wait for my child/grand-child to start school so they can learn to read. It was my mission then, as it is today, to teach, encourage, model, and urge parents to make reading their priority. As a former classroom teacher, parent of two, parent educator, and education consultant, I knew first-hand the impor-tance of reading in the home.

A person who does not read does not live up to his

true potential. Did you know that 800 million people around the world cannot read or write? Even to this day, there are homes and schools without books. Source: Inspiremykids.com

Reading has always been my passion. It was my emphasis as a student in school and later as a teacher in the classroom. So, get ready, buckle up, hold on, because I have a lot to share about how to get your kids to fall in love with reading.

Why is reading so important? Reading will shape who your children are and who they will become in the future. It is the foundation upon which everything else they learn will be built.

Whether you have already started reading at home with your children or you are unsure where to start, there is something in this chapter for everyone.

When you read to your children, you are building a legacy of excellence. Innately, kids love to be read to at all ages. As an adult, one of my favorite past times is enjoying a good book. When I packed for business travel, my audiobook collection was always a consideration..

At first, spending quality time reading and cuddling maybe appealing to your kids. Don't stop there. The more you read to them, will soon blossom into you reading with them.

Being my child's first teacher, creating a home that is my child's first school, and knowing that everything my child learns will hinge on how well he reads is why I'm sharing these literacy tips that are easily incorporated at home.

- Write your child a letter and ask for a written response.
- Allow your child to read the instructions when putting together toys and small appliances.
- Have your child write down phone messages.
- When eating out, ask your child to read the menu.
- Have them read traffic signs and billboards.
- Read labels on cereal and other packaged items.
- Speak in complete sentences when talking with your children. Encourage them to do the same.
- Engage your child in daily conversation.
- Use descriptive words to add to their shoebox.
- Underline descriptive words in magazines and newspapers.
- Allow your child to take gently used books, toys, and clothes to a shelter.
- Organize a family spelling bee.
- Create a family vision board.

Consistently engaging in the above activities is what I call seed planting. We have all heard the saying… good or bad, what you do often is what you will become. There was nothing on the above list that our children did not embrace. It doesn't matter where you start as long as you start. What are you waiting for?

In our active household, reading was a top priority. Conversations about reading and its importance were frequent topics. Convey to your children that reading is a lifestyle and those who read are more successful and get more enjoyment out of life.

Reading with a purpose will go a long way in keeping kids involved in reading. Tapping into what interest your child and making books accessible in those genres will work wonders. Your conversations will go from you need to read today, to what are you reading today?

Coby was our kid's first puppy. When the topic arose, reading a book about dogs was our first step before deciding what would be a good fit for our family. Hands down, the Pug won the vote. After learning that Pugs originated in China, Kelsi asked to name him Coby Chong to honor his heritage. We all agreed.

Learning about Pugs (Coby) via reading was fun, and whenever he did something out of character, the kids would say, "that wasn't what the book said he would do." They quickly learned that not all Pugs were the same.

Unfortunately, some of the parents in my seminars thought that teaching reading was the teacher's job. When you talk to your children, you are teaching them to read. After all, reading is making sense of words.

There is no special training needed, but you must be intentional about creating a reading culture in your home. Every home has a culture. It is what you value and how you spend your time. The culture that we created in our home was one of love and engagement. We didn't operate in separate spaces, and we valued our time together.

When we were not reading at home, we spent time browsing and reading in the library. The library still holds special memories for us, not just for the books, but also for the Saturday morning plays sponsored by the library and being read to by book characters dressed in full Disney habiliment. There wasn't a Disney book we didn't read or a Disney movie we didn't see.

Reading can bring families closer together. The more time you spend reading and telling stories, the stronger your family bond will be.

Allow your children to observe you reading books, newspapers, magazines, and even recipes. Discussing what you read will model for them to do the same. When kids know that a conversation will follow their reading, they will read with better comprehension.

To add value to reading, help your child see the connection between reading and writing. Try summarizing a story on paper or writing down the answers to a few key questions on index cards, starting with who, what, when, where, how, and why can work wonders. These activities will aid in developing better comprehension and more enjoyment.

As a parent educator, I was constantly reminding parents that reading is comprehension. I would ask, "how do you know if your child has understood what was read?"

For some parents observing their child reading or even listening to their child read was enough. Embarrassed, some parents would admit that this was the extent of reading in their homes. "Start small," I would say. Engage your child by asking questions while you are reading together. Talk about the book cover first, then point out the title, author, and illustrator. These are good ways to introduce new and interesting vocabulary words. Please encourage your child to start a list of new words as he reads.

This is a question that I was asked often during my parent seminars. "Should I allow my child to interrupt me with questions during our story time?" or "Should I have him wait until the end?"

"Be patient," I would say. When your child asks questions, that means he is paying attention. It would help if you encouraged even more conversation after you read.

Kids who read often generally will favor a particular genre of book. Henry Frank preferred a fantasy series, like Harry Potter and, later, Inheritance by Christopher Paolini. Like so many kids today, he followed an author's series. I never had to worry about him reading as long as his chosen authors would keep writing.

Books had a prominent place in our home year-round and would lay gift wrapped under the Christmas tree awaiting the big reveal. Admittedly, as their interest changed, it became safer to gift our kids with a Barnes and Noble gift card.

I recall the last gift card we gave Kelsi; she purchased an LSAT Study Guide during one of her summer breaks from college. She chose law school as her career path as early as third grade. I attribute her success as an attorney to her love for reading. Kelsi was a voracious reader who would read a book a week during her breaks from school. Currently, she is a leader of several book clubs focused on different genres.

What I know for sure...the key to raising kids to love reading starts with the parent's attitude toward reading. Our children will share our values. I kept books in our home and the back seat of the car. When we packed for vacation, which books to pack was a consideration.

By now, you have probably figured out that consistency is the key to developing in your children a love for reading.

Encouraging the older siblings to read to the younger ones will have many great rewards. Growing up as the youngest of six, I was constantly being read to. Playing school in our living room would keep the six of us entertained for hours. When we weren't playing school, we would play church. Now, that deserves its own chapter in a future book.

Just know that you are not alone. Your child's school, church, library, and community center may offer special programs focused on literacy. Use a search engine like arbookfind.com to find books on specific topics and genres at the appropriate difficulty level. This will also allow them to see how other kids have rated various books.

When your kids see what other kids like them are reading, it sparks their motivation to try something outside of their norm. Regardless of your child's grade level, arbookfind.com can show them the most popular books kids are reading at that grade level. Additionally, it shows which books have won which awards in your state.

Have your kids make up stories to exercise their creativity because what we do often is what we do well. The more they exercise their creativity, the more creative they will become. Later, please encourage them to write their stories down. Kids love reading their own stories well after they have written them. This will ignite more laughter and conversation than any author ever could accomplish.

When speaking to your children, refer to them as readers. Let them hear you say, "it is our family reading time!" Allow them to choose their books or stories to keep them motivated. Family reading time is an excellent time to introduce your children to poetry. Try making up words that rhyme. Say two sentences with words that rhyme at the end. Try saying one sentence, then ask your child to add a sentence that rhymes at the end. Keep it going.

A road trip is always a good time for playing word games. Our goal as parents was to enjoy the journey and not just pass the time. Our mantra was happy kids, happy life.

Here are a few of our family favorites: Some may require a simple notepad and pencil, but others will require no materials at all.

- A familiar favorite was the license plate game: count the different states on the license plate. Name that state's capital. Try to figure out what the initials mean on the license plates. Discuss which state you would like to visit on a future vacation and why.
- Count the number of red cars you see. Count the S.U.V.s. Ask the kids to come up with their own categories.
- Start a story chain. One person starts, and the next person contributes one or two lines. Everyone gets to add to the chain of events. These stories can be long or short, depending on the age of the child. This one is fun for your sophisticated teens as well.
- Have each child research the city or state where you are vacationing. The one with the most facts wins. Be sure to include some of the points of interest on the itinerary.
- Have plenty of books in the car for quiet time.
- Download books and games that are accessible without the internet.

I have shared a plethora of tips and strategies to help your kids fall in love with reading. Some of you may find this simple checklist easier to follow. If you can answer most of these with "yes," pat yourself on the back. You deserve it!

- I have different genres of books in my home.
- Our children see us reading something daily.
- I read aloud to my children daily.
- We read together as a family.
- My kids have a library card, and they use it.
- I ask my children questions as we read to check their understanding/comprehension.
- I allow my children to ask questions as I read to them.
- I encourage my children to write as they read – summaries, new word lists, what I liked about the story? Which character am I most like? If you could change the story, what would you change?
- I encourage my children to write thank-you notes, letters and make "to-do lists."
- I allow my child to make the grocery list, then check their list with a grocery receipt.
- My children have access to reference books and a dictionary at home.
- I allow my children to help me cook, paying particular attention to measuring and following directions.

- I purchase books, children magazine subscriptions, educational games, and puzzles for birthdays and holidays.
- I praise my children for wanting to read.
- I talk about what I'm reading, and I encourage my kids to do the same.
- I show interest in what my children are reading.

When I would say, "reading is comprehension, "it was sometimes an "aha moment" for parents attending my parent seminars. I would explain that some kids are good at decoding words, while others are good with fluency. So, what makes reading and comprehension synonymous? Simply put, if your child can not answer basic questions about what he has read or read to him, there is little or no understanding of the text. A child who understands or comprehends the text should be able to retell the story or at least recall the details. When you ask questions as you read to your children, you will quickly realize there may be an issue.

Try asking 3-4 of these questions each time you read with your child. Make it fun, as they have had a teacher at school all day. This is a good time for you to show some motherly love and encouragement. A few examples are given below:

- What is this story about?

- Did the pictures help you understand the story better?
- Who is telling the story?
- Do you agree with the title? How would you change it?
- Have you read books written by this author before?
- Do you have a favorite book written by this author?
- What was your favorite part of the story?
- Who is your favorite character?
- Why did you choose this book?
- What do you think is going to happen next?
- Is there a part of the story that you didn't understand?

Here are a few tips to try before asking the teacher for suggestions. Slow down when you are reading to your child. Read with expression to keep your child interested. Ask questions after reading a short passage. If you read too much before asking questions, your child may forget or become confused, mainly if there are many characters. There are many tools and programs that teachers can use to identify your child's appropriate reading level. Once you determine his or her "just right" reading level, allow your child to have many reading experiences at that level. They will let you know when they are ready for more of a challenge.

As you can see, learning to read is not enough. We

must help our children understand what they read or hear being read to them. Aforementioned, decoding and fluency are only parts of reading. At a foundational level, decoding is when your child sounds out words and syllables. Once decoding is mastered, fluency comes. Just keep reading, it's all part of the process. The more they hear someone reading to them, the easier decoding becomes. Fluency is when your child can read smoothly and at a good pace. They may slow down occasionally to decode or sound out a word, but a fluent reader will have better comprehension due to fewer stops.

Using flashcards and playing word games can make reading more fun and improve word recognition. Having a rich vocabulary is essential in helping our kids become good readers and fall in love with it. There are many ways to enhance your child's vocabulary. Besides reading daily, your everyday conversation is an excellent avenue for teaching language.

Start a tradition by introducing a new word each week. Have your child write it down on an index card along with the definition on the back. Challenge him to use it in your everyday conversations for a week before introducing a new word. We kept these index cards in a shoebox, and you guessed it…underneath their beds. This became one of our favorite family activities, reviewing these new and sometimes unusual words weeks and months later.

When the kids were younger, I was a member of my first book club. I would read about different cultures and faraway places that were sometimes difficult to find on a map. I would share my book discussions with the kids, saying to them, "the only thing better than reading a good book is talking about it with someone else." They witnessed the pure joy that radiated from me for days after my book club discussions.

One day out of nowhere, Kelsi suggested that we start a family book club. Everyone agreed. I encouraged the kids to create a plan that included who, what, when, where, how, and why. Impressed with their detailed planning, there was nothing left to do but execute the plan.

We started with a trip to the library. Everyone used their own library card. Unlike my adult book club, everyone chose their book to read and share in a book talk. Little did we know that we were preparing our children to become good public speakers. As they shared titles, authors, illustrators, characters, setting, plot, conflicts, and resolutions, we prepared our questions and comments. They would critique the author's work with likes and dislikes, deletions, and additions. Having a family book club was an adventure that taught us so much about each other. It was our family book club experience that led Kelsi to become an attorney. I thought Family Law would be her calling. She always wanted to help the underdog, the hurting children, and broken families.

It didn't take Henry Frank's choice of books for us to know that he would either be a career athlete or have a career in athletics.

So, drop everything and just read. Remember you

don't have to be perfect, but rather persistent in pursuing your goal to help your children become life-long readers who love to read.

Father, grant that our children will walk in love as Christ also hath loved us.

Ephesians 5:2 KJV

Adapted by the Author

CHAPTER FIVE

Family Game Night Reimagined

Outcomes

In this chapter, the parent/reader will discover how families playing games together can teach various skills and subjects while having fun.

"Play is often talked about as if it were a relief from serious learning. But for children, play is serious learning. Play is really the work of childhood."
Fred Rogers – Television personality

"The best inheritance a parent can give his children is a few minutes of his time each day."
Orlando Aloysius Battista – Canadian American Chemist and Author

Family game night can be a massive undertaking with tremendous rewards. The more you plan in advance the better the outcome. Start by surveying your children. Their input will be invaluable and set the stage for what may become your favorite family time together. The more children participate, the better to ensure a wide range of ideas and activities to choose from. The use of imagination was always on display during our game nights. Sometimes we would make up a game or activity on the fly. Occasionally a new hobby would emerge from our family engagement. Thinking outside the box comes easier with kids. Skywatching can be considered a game that may result in an interest in science. Photography allowed the children to explore nature at its best.

We collected books, games, cards, and puzzles. Some of our best finds came from a yard sale or a second-hand store.

Time wasn't always on our side. Bedtime would come before some games or puzzles were finished, giving us something to look forward to the next time. Monopoly would always become a multiple-day effort. Kelsi and Henry Frank's critical thinking and problem-solving skills were in full force. Truth be told, we never took pity on the children once they reached a certain age.

By the time they reached third grade, they were fierce and could hold their own during a board or card game.

Watching TV was not a priority for our children, especially during the week. As a relatively new mother, I learned, what you allow becomes their norm. The younger they are when you set family expectations, the happier your household will be. Some say happy wife happy life, but my experience has been happy kids happy life. The good news is that it doesn't take much to keep them happy. A survey was conducted many years ago, and kids were asked, "what do they want most from their parents?" The unanimous answer was TIME! Zig Ziglar even wrote the quote,

"To a child, love is spelled TIME."

Our children knew that we loved them, and they knew that we cared how they spent their time. Our love was shown through time and dedication and other intangible demonstrations of affection versus tangible gift giving. People who know us will be shocked to learn that our shopping for clothes and gifts were limited to birthdays, big holidays (Christmas and Easter), and back to school. Henry Frank still dwells on the fact that he never owned a play station as a child. I learned from the hundreds of parents and grandparents that play station is not for everyone. My philosophy was this, if it detracts from your schoolwork and family time, it's not for us. Before you feel sorry for him, he had plenty of exposure through friends and relatives. In fact, he became so skilled with it that no one believed he did not own one.

Our two Children were blessed with everything they needed and some of their wants. At the end of the day, our focus as parents was to spend quality time as a family and create unforgettable memories.

We could make the simplest things fun, like reading outside on a blanket or playing under the sprinklers wearing swimsuits.

Interviewing our children on a video recorder gave us something to relive and celebrate months later. It was terrific for them to see their physical and intellectual growth in real-time. In retrospect, we did not realize that we were shaping who they would become later in life. Many folks would agree, public speaking is the number one fear that people have. Thanks to those ongoing video interviews, Kelsi and Henry Frank are no strangers to public speaking. I have to also give our church (Mt. Pisgah

CME Church) kudos for providing numerous opportunities for them to speak publicly.

Our children were given many opportunities to perform as Worship Leaders for Children's and Young Adult Days. I also attribute their confident public delivery to the many Easter and Christmas speeches they delivered with excellent precision. In addition, they were summoned often to read the church announcements or introduce special guests.

A highlight for Henry Frank was when he introduced Reverend Jesse Jackson during his visit to Memphis to commemorate the 50th year memorial for Dr. Martin Luther King Jr., March 30, 2018.

Sometimes the games we play with our children can lead to a rewarding career. For example, as a child growing up in Pine Bluff, Arkansas, my siblings and I would play school to pass the time. I didn't realize it at the time, but those games and role-playing experiences led me to my 40-year career in education.

As an educator and entrepreneur, speaking publicly was in my will house. Fortunately, I have had over 40 years to perfect it.

Using the video camera was a fun way to help us all develop into great speakers in a non-partisan environment. Perfection wasn't the goal, but rather the joy of mirroring yourself on camera and the laughter that accompanied it was what mattered.

One of my retirement goals is to convert our many home videos onto a more modern media platform.

Generally speaking, our children were allowed to watch only one TV program/movie during the week and only if there were no sports practice, or dance, or band rehearsals, after school that day.

Involving them in positive and productive activities was the target. However, as parents we must help our children find their niche by exposing them to a wide range of opportunities. Ultimately, Kelsi excelled in music and Henry Frank in sports.

When your child searches for the niche, the best thing a parent can do is pay attention. Being observant during the game practices and band rehearsals is paramount. It always saddens me to see parents preoccupied with work or cell phones during these crucial times. Our kids need to know that what they are doing is important to us. They put forth more effort when we show that we care.

You will never regret the time you spend with your children. That time spent teaches us volumes about our children, likes, dislikes, strengths, and improvement areas.

Playing board games was one of my personal favorites after homework activities with the kids. It gave me a deeper insight into their personalities. Who was a good sport? Who was a gracious winner? Who was a gracious loser? Who was an encourager?

Playing games such as Monopoly, Life, Scrabble, Chess, Trivial Pursuit, Connect Four, Twister, Clue, Charades, and card games allowed us endless fun that provided brain stimulation, adventure, real world scenarios, problem solving strategies, and loads of fun memories.

Puzzles helped our kids develop their visual discrimination skills and enhance their attention to detail. It also required patience. The more puzzle pieces, the more mandatory patience became. We never shied away from a mega puzzle.

I knew the power of having books in our home. My end goal was to help Kelsi and Henry Frank fall in love with reading. Mission Accomplished! The stage was set for developing avid readers, one book at a time.

As a new mom, I didn't wait for the kids to arrive to begin reading to them. Instead, I read children's books as I massaged my protruding belly. It quickly became our nightly ritual. Henry did his part, as he knew the lights were not going out until our baby showed a sign of approval. Our routine seemed to soothe when there was an attempt to get my attention with a yarn or a kick.

Once they arrived, the nightly reading ritual continued. Never underestimate the benefits of reading to your infant children. The more they hear your voice, whether you are reading, speaking, or singing, it broadens their learning capacity.

We began pointing to the words with our toddlers as we read to them to demonstrate how reading starts at the top of the page and flows from left to right. They would memorize words and soon an entire book. Reading in our home was considered a fun activity like any other fun activity. Before long, they would start to recognize words by sight in other children's literature.

Reading bible stories or playing bible trivia was an engaging way to introduce our children to the word of God. Praying for your children and with your children is one of the most endearing acts a parent can show toward their children. Allow your children to hear you pray for them and teach them how to pray. Show them who God is by the way you live and treat others. When children understand why prayers are essential, they are more likely to understand and participate.

Make prayer a top priority in your home. Teach your children to say grace before meals and to pray each morning and night before bedtime.

You will never regret teaching your children about gratitude and being thankful. Help them start a "Gratitude Jar" at a young age. They will write down one thing a week on a post-it-note and place it in the jar. At the end of the month, pull out a few to review and reflect on all the good that has happened. This jar can evolve into a "Gratitude Journal" that can also be reviewed monthly.

To include our extended family and friends, we asked our Thanksgiving Dinner guests to write what they are thankful for in a beautifully decorated journal, which adorned the coffee table that couldn't be overlooked. It was not required, but no one ever turned down the opportunity to share.

It was pleasing for our returning guests to view what

they wrote the previous year(s) and collectively reflect on our many blessings.

Do you feel that your children watch too much TV? If your answer is yes, it's never too late to change family habits. Kids crave the attention of their parents and are naturally creative. When given a choice, they will choose to spend time with us doing something fun and engaging.

Try playing a card game on a blanket in the backyard or on the front porch. Don't forget the snacks!

Most children have an innate ability to role-play. If acting out a character in a book doesn't spark interest, try charades. This allows them to use those hidden talents that a book character may not convey.

Animal Charades was something we could all agree upon. Allowing our kids to showcase their knowledge of animals and depth of creativity. Two things both of them had a fair share of. "It's not easy to distinguish the difference between a Jaguar, Leopard, and a Cheetah," Kelsi would exclaim. I was always in awe to hear Henry Frank describe the differences. Sometimes his depth of animal knowledge would leave us all speechless.

Another fun way to spend family time together is storytelling. Whether made up or true, telling stories can be passed down for many generations.

This is also an opportunity to debunk old wives tales or myths, like black cats and Friday the 13th are bad luck. They would giggle at the one about pulling out a gray hair, and two more would grow to replace it. This would ignite a conversation about which of their teachers pulled out gray hair more often.

They chose to believe this one. Find a penny, pick it up, all that day will bring good luck. When someone would comment, "it's just a penny," they would giggle as they pocketed the penny.

I mentioned in an earlier chapter how sharing childhood memories through storytelling is so powerful. These stories provide an avenue of trust and relatability. During my extensive work with parents and grandparents, I would glean a lack of communication between parents/grandparents and children. I repeatedly heard from both how their children felt misunderstood by them.

Storytelling is a great way to open the door to who we were at their age. The more they know about you then, the more interested they will be in who you are now.

Try playing a game that you played as a child with your children. Do your children know what "jacks" are? What about a "spinning top" or a "yoyo?" These toys of yesteryear may prove difficult to locate. I could always rely on Cracker Barrel Store for vintage games and toys.

Being spontaneous can stir creativity and peek curiosity. Try randomly asking what comes after 99 and before 107? Or how many words can you create using the letters in COMPUTER or FAMILY?

Throughout this chapter, I have shared a wealth of games and activities to increase engagement while spending quality time as a family. The skills, subjects, and knowledge of each other while spending family time is immeasurable.

Here are some additional classics you will want to incorporate along the way:

- Play a family game of dominos.
- Play a family game of bingo.
- Play a family game of Simon Said.
- Play a family guessing game.

If you can handle the truth, try this final suggestion:

- Have each family member describe the family by drawing a line down the center of a legal pad. Label one side "Pros" and the other "Cons." Explain the difference or use "Likes" and "Dislikes" for age appropriateness. Everyone shares their list without any complaints from others. Each person will choose one thing they can improve on. Revisit the list every other month or so and watch your family bond soar!

The important thing is to get started. Choose a few games, or better yet, allow your children to choose. Your focus should be persistence, not perfection. Learn to laugh at your own mistakes and those of your children. Keep things light. Before you can exhale, your children will be leaving home for college or a career. Create memories that your children will be proud of and want to mimic with their children. What I know for sure...parents will never regret the time they invest in their family.

Heavenly Father, grant that my children would be filled with joy given by the Holy Spirit.
1 Thessalonians 1:6 KJV

Adapted by the Author

CHAPTER SIX

Strategies for Managing and Resolving Conflict

Outcomes

In this chapter, the parent/reader will examine tips and strategies to assist their children with managing and resolving conflict and becoming better problem-solvers.

"Children have never been good at listening to their elders, but they have never failed to imitate them."
James Baldwin - Author and Activist

"It is easier to build strong children than to repair broken men."
Frederick Douglass - American Abolitionist, Orator and Writer

All of us experience conflict in our lives. Even as adults, we are constantly searching for ways to resolve disputes and become better problem solvers. This chapter is sure to provide tips and strategies for children and parents alike.

Although we try to avoid conflict, it happens in every area of our lives. Whether it's in our families, on our jobs, among our peers, in our church, our community, politics, or the world, conflict is ever-present.

According to Wikipedia, a conflict is a clash of interests. The basis of conflict may vary, but it is always a part of society. Basis of conflict may be personal, racial, class, caste, political, and international.

In my words, conflict is a disagreement that may not easily be resolved. However, many conflicts can be resolved, but it will take some effort from all parties involved.

Why deal with it if it's so unpleasant? Solving a problem or resolving a conflict is imperative because no one wins when it's left unsolved or unresolved.

When it comes to managing conflict, we are all unique in our approach; however, the core procedure can be the same. So, where do we start?

We start with open and honest communication. Remember, our children will be more like us than unlike us. This kind of communication helps us be more intentional in our response when we are angry with someone or something.

Practicing these two things will help build the skills we need for this never-ending journey.

- Talk about what's bothering you as calmly as possible. When we model having a cool head amid conflict or disagreement, we set the stage for how our children will deal with conflict or disagreement.
- Practice talking through conflict with your children. Refrain from trying to fix the problem for your child. The end goal is to teach them how to manage their conflicts and become better problem solvers. When children learn to cooperate with others at

home, school, church, sports, or other extracurricular activities, they understand the life skills of solving problems and managing conflict.

As parents, we must equip ourselves with helpful strategies so that we are helping and not hurting our children.

Here are a few things that we should steer away from when teaching our children how to keep a cool head in the midst of conflict:

- Don't take over; include your child in solving problems and resolving conflict. Discuss options for what course of action should be taken. This will show that you have confidence in their decision.
- Don't overemphasize mistakes your child may have made. Remember that they are children learning to navigate through a difficult situation. Let them know that you love them despite a mistake they may have made.
- Don't demand more of your child than they are capable of delivering. Be sure that your approach in teaching your child how to resolve conflict is age-appropriate.
- Don't allow your children to watch violence on television or at the movies. Children process things differently than adults and may think

that violence is ok since you enable them to view it in your home.

- Never excuse or encourage fighting or bullying to resolve conflict. Try this, practice counting to ten before responding when you are angry and teach your child to do the same. This ten-second pause will allow you to gain perspective.

Children are not born undisciplined. It's what they see and hear in the environment in which they live and spent time in that will shape their level of self-control.

Are you an "Active Listener?" Are you teaching your children to be an "Active Listener?" Many problems or conflicts can be resolved through "Active Listening." This may be easier said than done because we are generally more focused on being heard than hearing the other person's point of view.

I give credit to our family meetings for providing an avenue for us to practice this technique as a family.

Here are a few active listening techniques you can practice with your family. First, set a few ground rules:

- Each person gets to speak without interruption.
- All eyes on the person speaking.
- No distractions allowed (television, cell phone, iPad, laptop, etc.).
- Before responding, you must repeat what the

person just stated. This will clear up any misunderstandings before they start.

Sometimes during our family meetings, as parents, we would discuss our difficulties in managing conflict. This allowed us to get input from our children on how they would handle certain situations if it were them. We would discuss the pros and cons of our actions.

This short survey was published by (The Parent Institute, 2002). The purpose is to ensure that we are not raising bullies while they are learning to manage conflict. Answer "yes" or "no" to the seven questions below.

- Are hitting, cursing, and harassment allowed in your home?
- Do I allow my child to watch violence on television or in movies?
- Do I accept aggressive behavior as normal and expected?
- Do I enable conflicts to go unresolved so that anger builds up?
- Do I allow my child to tease or hurt our pet or other animals?
- Do I discipline my child by making threats?
- Do I avoid expressing love and affection for my child?

How did you score?

If you answered YES to any of the above questions, look at your child's behavior. Consider whether or not you are creating an environment in your home that fosters bullying.

When your house rules allow for an even exchange like, taking turns and open communication, you can expect everyone to handle conflict better.

These are things that we would try when conflict arose:

- Sending the children to their rooms to gain some perspective worked for us because there was no television or play station in their rooms to distract them.
- Treating our children with respect let them know that despite the conflict, we still loved them.
- Avoid name-calling, blaming, and making excuses.
- Work on a solution together. Include everyone involved.
- Follow through on the agreed-upon solution.

The more we involve our children in managing conflict and solving problems, the more skilled at doing these things they will become.

Start early with simple problems like what to wear to school? How much of your allowance should be saved to pay for a toy? Who do you want to become friends with and why? When children are able to solve problems for themselves, they will gain confidence and have greater success in life. They will experience less anxiety when they feel in control of their lives.

Don't forget to have your children make a list of chores needed around the house. Let them choose their tasks. Ask them how often should that chore be performed? Do you agree? If not, continue the conversation until everyone agrees. Their allowance should match the chore. If someone steps up to do more, their budget should be more. This is an excellent life lesson to teach—the more responsibility, the bigger the reward.

Children are born solving problems. When an infant rolls over for the first time, they have solved the problem of laying on their back. Just think of the problem-solving that goes into crawling or taking the first step. With every problem solved, they are building more confidence for handling bigger challenges.

Managing conflict and solving problems are a part of life. As parents, we can emphasize that someone had to solve a problem for us to have the basic necessities of life. What we eat, the clothes we wear, where we live, the toys that we have all started with a thought first. Someone had to begin solving problems to bring it all to fruition.

Praise is the key when our children demonstrate good problem-solving skills. The more we praise them for making good decisions, the better problem solvers they will become.

Playing board games or card games is an excellent

way for your child to showcase the kind of problem-solver they are becoming. It's also a great avenue to witness how well they manage conflict. This is a good time to teach them that you don't always have to agree. It's good to have another way to solve the same problem. Please encourage your child to ask questions of themselves and others.

Practice asking them open-ended questions that require a thought-filled response.

Here are a few examples:

- What is the problem that needs to be solved?
- How have similar problems been solved?
- Where should I start to solve the problem?
- Is there a process I can use?
- How long will it take to solve the problem?

Write down your plan. Tweak it as you go, if needed. Sometimes asking the right questions will make the solution easier.

Teach your kids to be curious by asking them what they think. Follow up with, "that was a smart answer." What do you say when your child responds incorrectly? The goal is to leave your child with his self-esteem intact. A few things you may say, "no one is right all of the time." "Let's think this through together."

This may be a great time to teach tolerance of others' points of view. Share some examples of when you disagreed with a friend or a boss. Discuss how you handled these conflicts. Some conflicts are derived from people having beliefs and life experiences other than your own.

This could be a double-edge sword, in that, your point of view may need to be tolerated by others. Sometimes we have to learn to agree to disagree and move forward with the things we can control.

When we teach our children to have a positive attitude towards life, they are more tolerant of others and their opposing viewpoints.

Tolerance is taught in the home. Families disagree all the time. It's how we model a spirit of patience, cooperation, and even forgiveness that will guide our children's life-long lessons of solving problems and managing conflict appropriately.

Tolerance is a verb. It requires action. I have a saying that I used when instructing teachers and parents. "None of us is as smart as all of us." This reigns true in our home, at work, and among our peers.

Cooperation and working together are what strong families are built upon. I have seen and heard of many families not cooperating or working together. This is one of the reasons that I'm so passionate about writing this book. I don't know of any families who set out to be uncooperative and not working together. In most cases, when we learn better, we do better. It's never too late to improve family relationships.

Let's learn more about families working together to strengthen the family bond. As parents, my husband and

I presented a united front when teaching our kids how to work well together. Next, we taught them how to work well with others. We believe that charity begins at home.

When we show love for our children and do not take sides, they will be more cooperative and tolerant of each other. This takes patience on the part of everyone in the home. When we keep things light and learn to laugh at ourselves, we have fewer conflicts and more cooperation.

The better your children feel about themselves and their contribution to a process, the easier it will be for them to work cooperatively with others. The level of their self-esteem will help them see the value they have added. Self-esteem and self-respect are synonymous. As we teach our children to respect themselves, us, and others, we must show our respect for them. They need to know that their opinions and ideas matter.

Self-esteem is directly tied to how our children will handle problems, manage conflict, and cooperate with others. Children with high self-esteem have a "yes I can" attitude. They are not afraid to try a new sport, meet new people, or tackle a challenging assignment at school.

Remember that every child is unique, there are no cookie-cutter kids. They all come to us as a gift from God, uniquely wrapped. As parents, it is our responsibility to help them unwrap the gift inside of them. We can start unwrapping the gifts that they are by affirming who they are.

This happens when they hear us say:

- I respect your choices.
- I like the way you handled that.
- I thank God for you.
- Thank you for allowing your brother to go first when it was your turn.
- You are a blessing to our family.
- I like the way you all show love for each other.
- Thank you for being so polite.
- You make us proud.
- Thank you for telling the truth.
- You don't lose until you stop trying.

Let this be the language of love that echoes throughout your home.

We cannot avoid problems in life, it is all a part of living. What's important is how we resolve the issues we face from time to time and how well we work with others in the process.

God, strengthen my children with all power so that they may have great endurance and patience.

Galatians 5:22 KJV

Adapted by the Author

CHAPTER SEVEN

Strategies for Teaching Math at Home – No Problem

Outcomes

In this chapter, the parent/reader will explore teaching strategies and reinforce various math concepts during family time together.

> *"A person who never made a mistake never tried anything new."*
> Albert Einstein - Theoretical Physicist and Nobel Prize Winner

> *"If you stop at general math, then you will make general money."*
> Snoop Dogg - American Rapper and Music Producer

I am my child's first teacher. My home is my child's first school. Math is as important as reading. You can't do one well without the other. I remember telling our kids how important math is. I was on a mission to demonstrate that not a day goes by when math is not needed. They were able to see firsthand how math was a part of everyday life. When I made math fun at home, I quickly realized our children performed better with math at school.

No one will dispute that of all the subjects in school, math has evolved the most. But, no matter how you teach it, math is still math.

During my parenting seminars, I would say to the parents, "all you need to encourage math at home is a positive attitude." Some parents and teachers feel that math is the most challenging one to teach of all the subjects.

I contend the key is to make math fun. Remember the neighborhood walks that I referenced in an earlier chapter? Whether we were walking in the community or at the walking trail, we did more than walk; we did the math. The kids learned early that counting birds, trees, squirrels, or an occasional rabbit made our walks an adventure. "Who knew that counting could be so much fun," the kids would say.

They felt smart when I introduced them to geometry. Our kids would look for as many geometric shapes as possible, circles, squares, rectangles, triangles, hexagons, and octagons, you name it. This increased curiosity with math turned their attention from trees and animals to houses, buildings, and windows.

Our pizza nights were always filled with math jargon. We would challenge the children to figure out what percentage each of us ate. This wasn't an easy task since we all ate different portions. Even as toddlers, I would reward the kids with as many cheerios or raisins as they could count. I could literally see their thoughts, as their ability to count increased with every snack time.

One of their first educational toys was a wooden abacus. It provided numerous fun ways to teach numbers, colors, patterns, addition, subtraction, multiplication, basic division, and more. For example, after they learned to count on their fingers, I would ask them to show me what 12 looks like using the abacus. Before long, we were exploring a bigger number.

Kelsi introduced Henry Frank to the abacus when he was one year old and she was four and a half. I was confident that Kelsi would follow in my footsteps and become an educator. However, it was much later that I realized that she just liked being in charge. When Henry Frank figured out her motive, he decided he needed his independence and could learn without her instructions.

One of our favorites "math at home" activities was grocery shopping. Math class was always in session when it was my turn to bring the class snack or the soccer team drinks. Our children were clever enough to figure out what was needed for the class or the team and still have a surplus for our home.

Using the scale in the grocery store's produce section provided many opportunities to teach and reinforce the complex math skill, estimation. I would ask the kids to guess the weight of the apples we were purchasing. Then, based on the cost per pound, they would try to estimate the dollar amount. This sophisticated math skill would draw a small audience around the scale when the kids would make their predictions.

All kids need praise from folks other than their parents. So having my toddlers count as high as they could count for their grandparents, aunts, and uncles provided the stage they needed to show off their smarts.

Later, they would recite for family members, mental math addition with 2-digits or more. Their mastery of multiplication facts would earn them coins and hugs. Sometimes I would ask silly questions like, "how old would your dad be if you added all of our ages together?" This would sometimes require a pencil and paper. It was also a way to track everyone's age.

Card games don't just enhance reading and problem-solving skills. They also help to improve the stamina needed to become good at math. For example, we would use index cards with a number on one side placed faced down and spread out on the floor. Each of us would pick up two cards and add the two numbers. Everyone received a point for a correct response. This could also become a matching game that required memory of where the matching number was located.

We learned to laugh at our mistakes and have fun.

When our children were introduced to measurements, they measured everything. They were like little detectives, combing the house with pen and paper in hand. Using a ruler, they would measure their books, their toys, pots, and pans. Graduating to the measuring tape allowed them to measure more significant items like tables and chairs and even each other. Their height charts still grace the door frames of their bedrooms all these years later.

It is never too early to allow your children to see you balance your checkbook. We would discuss how making deposits involved adding and making withdrawals involved subtracting. We had a saying in our home, "no money in means no money out."

Everyone had a job to do. Henry and I had the job of

earning a living via our chosen professions, while our children had the job of attending school and earning good grades.

They loved hearing their dad and me reminisce over our college days. The expectation was that Kelsi and Henry Frank would attend a college of their choice. They were also expected to assist us in financing their college education by making the kind of grades that would earn them scholarships to defray our cost.

What I have learned over the years, when you raise the bar for your children, they will rise to the occasion. Sometimes in their own time and their own way, but they will rise.

One of the frequently asked questions I'd receive from teachers and parents alike was my opinion regarding the use of calculators. I would reply, "there is a place and time for calculator usage. However, the most important thing of all is to ensure that our children have the ability to do some mental math. Having a working knowledge of addition, subtraction, multiplication, and division will help your child to know if the calculator's answer is reasonable."

There is no shortcut to learning math facts. Just like for you and me, math facts require practice, practice, practice.

Are you doing enough to promote math in your home? If you can say yes to many of these suggestions, then the answer is yes, you are.

Put a checkmark next to each suggestion that depicts your family's math engagement.

- I allow my children to take turns adding up our grocery costs as we shop.
- I ask my children, "how will the taxes in our state change the total?"
- My children add up the numbers on license plates of passing vehicles to see who gets the highest number.
- We read books about numbers.
- We study maps together and discuss the sizes of cities, states, and countries.
- My children have a good sense of which cities and states are located to our north, south, east, and west.
- We research the population and demographics of places we travel to or through.
- We talk about how much time it takes to drive vs. fly and the advantages of both.
- We discuss measurements and fractions while cooking together
- We discuss the amount of savings when something goes on sale.
- My children are encouraged to save a certain percentage of their allowance.

One of my favorite things to do to pass the time was to create random word problems for the children. Things like, if you were carrying a bag containing 75 oranges and the bag broke, causing you to lose 15 of them, how many oranges would you have left? Eventually, they would try and stomp their dad and me with their own word problems.

When children become good problem solvers in general, they perform better with word problems. Figuring out word problems can be a bit challenging.

Here are a few things to remember:

1. Figure out what question needs to be answered.
2. What information is needed to solve the problem.
3. What steps need to be followed. Devise a plan.
4. Begin solving the problem.
5. Double-check your work by answering the following questions. Did you answer the problem completely? Does your answer make sense?

Once your children realize the importance of math in everyday life, they will work harder to understand it better. So, when we have a positive attitude about math and the role that it plays in our lives, our children will reflect that same attitude toward math.

When you make it fun, they won't realize that they are becoming better at math and word problems. Occasionally, ask them to estimate the number of miles it takes to get to band rehearsal in 15 minutes or football practice in 20 minutes? What about the number of minutes vs. miles? Will taking the interstate change the minutes? Why? Will it change the miles? Why?

The more we can connect math to the real world, the better, like having conversations about your bills and what it takes to live. Discuss how your mortgage payment works. Please make a list of household bills with your kids so that they can get a sense of how much money it takes to live as you do.

It's important to avoid stereotypes when it comes to math. Instead, encourage your girls and boys to excel in math. Let them both know that anyone who works hard can be good at whatever they set their minds to.

When it comes to birthdays and holidays, think, "math." Start them out with educational counting toys such as building blocks, math link cubes, counting bears with matching sorting cups, number puzzles, Legos, and my personal favorite, the 100 beads abacus.

When you take the time to gift wrap an educational toy or game, that speaks volumes to a child about its importance. The younger they are when receiving these types of gifts, the better. Children will love what comes gift wrapped, especially when you spent time reading the books to and with them or explaining how to work the game or toy. If they see the gift as a magnet that draws you closer to them, everyone wins.

With a bit of imagination, you can turn just about any game into a math game. For example, try playing checkers using multiplication facts. The person who answers the math fact correctly gets to make a move on the checkerboard. If you answer incorrectly, you lose a turn.

Encourage your kids to make up math games. You will be surprised at their creative imaginations. Let your kids know about their budget before going to a restaurant. If their order goes over the budgeted amount, that overage is subtracted from their allowance.

Math can be used to determine the difference in the temperature from day to night and from night to day. So, when planning for the weekend, allow your children to track the weather all week long.

Graphs can be a fun and informative way to encourage the use of math at home. For example, using a bar graph, you can track the height of everyone in the family, including relatives.

Kids love to monitor the growth of things that they have planted. Use a small container to get them planting beans or seeds. Set the container on the window seal and have your kids chart the growth.

Graphs can be used to chart a child's allowance and savings. Setting a savings goal can motivate your child to save more and encourage more focus on math in general.

The more you apply math to everyday life, the more you will "multiply" your child's chances of succeeding with math at home, at school, and in life.

. . .

Lord, teach our children to persevere in all they do and help them run with perseverance the race set before them.

Hebrew 12:1 KJV

Adapted by the Author

CHAPTER EIGHT

Don't Stress the Small Stuff

Outcomes

In this chapter, the parent/reader will learn to identify stress factors and discover strategies for managing stress for themselves and their children.

"Children are like wet cement; whatever falls on them makes an impression."

Haim Ginott - Child Psychologist

"Treat a child as though he is already the person he's capable of becoming."

Haim Ginott - Child Psychologist

"Forgiveness can be the beginning of reducing stress in our lives. We must remember that hatred is like acid.

It does more damage to the vessel in which it's stored than the object on which it's poured. "

Ann Landers - Syndicated Advice Columnist

Let's start with this question. What is Stress? According to www.verywellmind.com, stress can be defined as any change that causes physical, emotional, or psychological strain. Stress is your body's response to anything that requires attention or action. Everyone experiences stress to some degree.

The difference is how well we are equipped to handle

it. Different stressors can bring on other reactions. For a parent, it could be a promotion at work. A promotion could bring on stress fueled by motivation. Even though the upgrade may result in substantial personal or professional growth, it can still be a stressful experience.

As a parent, a drastic change, even a good one, can bring on an emotional, physical, or psychological strain. When we realize that stress is a part of life and we all experience it, we can use the stress in the above example to motivate us and excel in our new position at work.

Adversely, if a parent experiences a dreadful life-changing event, stress can be fueled by anxiety. Just like stress, we all feel anxious at times. When anxiety interferes with our daily lives frequently, it's time to learn how to manage our stress.

Stress has no respecter of persons. Children can experience stress as well. Children can feel the same emotional, physical, or psychological strain. Imagine the stress that our children feel when competing for the first chair in the school band or a specific position in the year's biggest football game.

Stress factors can derive from family, friends, school, or even from the children themselves. As parents, we can help our children manage their stress with a few simple strategies.

First, try to reduce the amount of stress in your home by:

- Being a good listener. When your children are

trying to express themselves, stop what you are doing and listen. Children build high self-esteem when they know what they think matter.

- Showing love and affection toward your children. No matter the age, hugs do matter.

- Acknowledging your children's feelings. If they are afraid of something or someone, find out why. If appropriate, reassure them of their safety.

- Not over-scheduling your children with too many activities. Please help them to choose one or two. Teach them to finish what they start. When that season or activity is over, allow them to try something new. Don't push them to try activities that you like. Let them choose.

- Developing trust and allow your children to make mistakes. Please help them to see that mistakes are opportunities to learn.

- Being supportive. Allow your children to solve his or her problems, when appropriate. If your help is needed, don't take over. Teach them to be a part of the solution. Solving problems behind their backs teach them nothing.

- Having clear expectations without being too rigid. Give your children permission to be kids and have fun.

Secondly, help your children develop positive coping skills by:

- Setting a good example. When things go awry, as they sometimes do, stay calm. Model for your children how to resolve conflict peacefully, even when they are angry.
- Teaching your children that good and bad consequences are based on good and bad choices. Instill good values within your children so that they will know right from wrong.
- Allowing your children to make some decisions within the family structure. Start with what to wear to school. If you don't purchase inappropriate clothing, you won't have to worry that they will choose inappropriately. Also, allow your children to determine the family activity for family night. Have them organize it and explain everyone's role.
- Teaching your kids to be good sports, even when they are losing. Model good sportsmanship when things don't go your way. When our children know that no one wins every time, they are better equipped to handle losing, occasionally.

Lastly, help your children get the stress out by:

- Finding fun and practical ways to let off steam. Regular exercise is one of the best ways to reduce stress. For children, it can mean playing a sport that requires movement. Exercising the brain by reading a book or putting a puzzle together are additional ways to let off steam. We were intentional about helping our kids fall in love with nature. We didn't realize it at the time but, those daily walks after dinner were stress relievers. Bike-riding and skating were great alternatives for walking. Too much of the same thing can become tiresome. The key was to allow them to have choices.
- Getting your children involved in community service projects early. Volunteer work that helps others can reduce stress in children and adults. When you provide a service for others, you have little time to focus on what is bothering you. A hobby can also help your child feel more relaxed.
- Telling jokes as a family; everyone can join in the laughter.

I believe laughter is the best medicine. I am grateful that my husband and I have a sense of humor. When there is a lot of laughter in your home, things feel lighter and brighter. Start with a few knock-knock jokes and see how creative your children will become.

- Encouraging journal writing. Journal writing is not just for girls. It was called a diary when I was growing up. Either way, writing about your thoughts and feelings can be very therapeutic. When your children are too young to express their thoughts in writing, encourage them to draw a picture to depict how they feel. When they are sharing why they drew the picture, they are actually describing how they feel.
- Encouraging conversations about feelings, whether good or bad. Simply listening to your children can help them get the stress relief they need. Always end these conversations with a hug and don't forget to thank them for sharing these private moments with you.

Be observant about what is normal behavior for your kids so that abnormal behavior is easily identified.

Your children may not tell you that they feel stressed, but there are some signs to look for.

- Loss of appetite for some children is a clear sign of stress; however, overeating could be a sign for others.
- Upset stomachs or headaches could be indications of stress in our children. There is nothing wrong with asking your child, "is

anything bothering, worrying, or stressing
you?"

- Nightmares could be a symptom of stress as
  well as trouble falling asleep. If your child
  suddenly wants to sleep with you, this may be
  a sign of stress caused by fear. New or
  recurring fears could be other signs of stress,
  like the fear of strangers, fear of being alone,
  or fear of the dark.

- Sometimes we can mistake bad or stubborn
  behavior with defiance, but this could result
  from stress.

Why is it important for parents to learn about stress?
The answer is two-fold. Stress can be a motivator, but too
much stress can be harmful. It can give our children and
us the fuel we need to meet life's challenges when it works
as a motivator. When stress is a motivator it can get us
through that job promotion. It can also motivate our children to compete in a spelling bee. Adversely, too much
stress can fuel our anxiety. This is a harmful level of
stress. A large amount of stress can wear us down and
manifest itself as a physical, emotional, or psychological
problem.

According to research conducted by The Bacchus
Network, 2006, as life has gotten faster and more
demanding, it is not the physical challenges that we seem
most at risk for but the emotional and psychological ones.
Stress has been called the nation's number one health

problem – for a good reason. Almost 75% of people report being under "great stress," at least one day a week. It is estimated that 75% – 90% of all visits to physicians are due to stress-related problems. Stress has become a factor in everyday life.

Even though stress may differ for parents and children, stress is a part of life. It may not always be detrimental, but it is unavoidable. At its best, stress can provide us with the fuel we need to pursue our goals in life. I can recall several occasions in my own life when stress propelled me to take a giant step in my career.

As much as I loved teaching in a classroom setting, I was stressed. I struggled to make ends meet as a classroom teacher in Arkansas in the early '80s. Stress played a pivotal role in my life when I left my teaching career in Arkansas to join an Educational Software Company, which relocated me to Tennessee.

I call it "good stress," when it motivates me to try something new and different with a positive result. "Good Stress" played another pivotal role in my life when after 17 years with my first company, I decided I had what it took to become an entrepreneur.

What I quickly learned in both instances, sometimes we trade one stressor for another. Leaving the classroom solved my financial woes, but adjusting to corporate America introduced me to a new stress level. Working in corporate America taught me that the bottom line was first and people were second. Lucky for me, I was a high achiever, and when it came to my work, failure was not an option.

It is easy to excel when you enjoy what you do. My first company after leaving the classroom is where I began my work as a Parent Educator. This company did not actually offer a viable parental involvement component. Due to high customer demand, my company allowed me to create such a component. I began to research the topics requested by these customers. Because of the nature of my work, creating seminars around these topics came naturally to me. Before long, I was selling and delivering these custom seminars. Needless to say, my work was well received by the customer/school district, which was ranked one of the largest in the nation at that time.

I wore many hats for this company, but my newfound love was my extensive parental engagement work. I also continued to provide high level professional development for teachers, which I still enjoyed. Someone once told me that you are willing to do the work for free when you find your true passion.

I decided if I could develop an entire parental involvement component, sell it, and deliver it for a highly-regarded Educational Instructional Software Company, it may be worth the stress of venturing out on my own. I did just that.

Was it stressful? Yes! Was it worth it? Hell Yes! I consider my ten years as President and CEO of Brenda Reed Pilcher, Educational Consulting Services, the highlight of my 40 years in the education field.

It was liberating to get up each day, knowing the services I delivered reflected my company and me. The buck started and stopped with me. I was up for the challenge, stress and all. Personally, I dealt with stress through prayer and meditation. It's crucial to establish a routine to de-stress. When stress is not dealt with appropriately, it can begin to affect us in negative ways. Walking was my exercise of choice and remains my number one physical de-stressor. When my heart beats faster, or my muscles get tense, I know it's time for some deep breathing exercises. This was my sure-fire way to slow down my heart rate and release tension in my muscles.

Many years ago, I was introduced to the "Body Scan," a relaxation technique. Google it and find a version that suits you.

Parents need to know that being a parent can be stressful. The day-to-day routine of parenting can sometimes weigh heavily on us.

Whether you are a stay-at-home parent or have a career, you must learn to manage stress as a way of life. When a parent is under pressure, it can affect the whole family.

Here are a few signs to watch for:

- Frequent illnesses like headaches and stomach aches
- Short-tempered is a sign of stress. A parent may use inappropriate language or lash out at his or her child.

- Depression can weaken your ability to care for your children or your home. If you have a feeling of hopelessness, it is time to get help.
- Stop reinforcing the children's daily routine, such as getting to bed at a particular time, household chores, eating meals as a family, or leaving for school on time.

One of the most important steps a parent can take is to learn to manage stress. Remember, the children will learn coping strategies that you use when handling stress or stressful situations.

Here are a few tips to try. Find what works best for you:

- Identify your stressors. We all feel frustrated or angry at times. When you recognize your feelings, you can gain control. Try to pinpoint who, when, and where these stressors occur.
- Walking, praying, meditating, or deep breathing may work for some of us. Getting lost in a good book or a warm bath may work for others.
- Be patient with yourself. Expect to make mistakes now and then and try to learn from them. As long as you keep looking for a solution, you will eventually learn to manage your stress.
- Maintain a healthy diet and get 7 – 8 hours of

sleep. Being rested will help you deal with your children more patiently, especially during stressful situations.

Lastly,

- Get help if necessary. There is nothing wrong with reaching out for support. Talk to a family member or a close friend. Look into community resources. Take a break from the children by allowing your spouse or a trusted friend to watch the children for one hour a week.

Do you have strong stress-management skills?

Answer "yes" or "no" to the following to find out where you stand:

- Do you have trouble following through with your plans?
- Do you feel you have control over your life?
- Can you relax when tension starts to build?
- Do you like your job?
- Do you feel burned out by your job?
- Are most of your time spent on burdens and responsibilities?
- Do distractions keep you from doing what you want?
- Are you a passionate person?

- Have you added a child to your household, married, or changed jobs within the last year?
- Is your health in the good-to-excellent range?
- Is there any stress in your life that you think is helpful?
- Do you feel guilty about taking time for yourself?

There is no doubt that a few of these answers should be "no." If you answered these stress questions with more "yes" than "no" answers, you have strong stress-management skills.

As a parent, don't allow stress to get the best of you. We are all in this together. Be in the know.

S – Stay calm

T – Talk to a professional

R – Read to relax

E – Educate yourself if you feel overly stressed

S – Start an exercise routine

S – Stress can be helpful

Father God, help my children make every effort to do what leads to peace.

Romans 14:19 KJV

Adapted by the Author

CHAPTER NINE

*Parents Promoting Writing:
Keeping Writing Relevant*

Outcomes

In this chapter, the parent/reader will uncover why writing is one of the most critical skills for children to learn. They will also explore ways to keep writing relevant.

"If there is a book that you want to read, but it hasn't been written yet, then you must write it."

Toni Morrison – Author and College Professor

"You don't write because you want to say something; you write because you have something to say."

F. Scott Fitzgerald - American Novelist and Screenwriter

Do your children love to write? If the answer is no, don't worry, it is not too late to help them fall in love with this vital skill. So many parents and children don't realize how being a good writer can impact your quality of life. It's just that important.

By the end of this chapter, and after you have implemented a few of these writing strategies with your children, one or two things can happen.

1. Your child will discover a newfound love for writing.

2. Your child will realize the importance of writing in shaping who they will ultimately become in life.

Did you know that without writing, there would be no reading? Think about it; someone had to sit down and write all the books we love to read. That's why writing and reading are the two most critical skills our children can learn in school.

We all know that reading requires practice. Furthermore, the more our children practice writing, the better writer they will become. This important skill can determine what grade they will receive in school. Many colleges require a writing sample before admission is approved. Even a job application cannot be completed without the ability to write. There are very few occupations that don't require some form of written communication.

Parents can play a critical role in helping their children develop as writers. For example, when they see you writing a thank you letter to a friend or relative, you are modeling the importance of written communication.

Everyone loves to receive a thank you card or note, but it's the handwritten ones that mean the most. Why? Everyone knows that it takes time, effort, and gratitude to sit down and compose a handwritten note.

By helping your children write a thank you note, you are teaching them the meaning of gratitude. Children are not born selfish; it's what they see and are taught that shapes their responses. So, the next time your children receive a birthday or Christmas gift or a random act of kindness gift, use these occasions to start a writing craze.

The school or public library are great resources for writing opportunities. Kelsi our eldest, began her poem submissions for publication in second and third grades. Teachers can be a great motivator for children who show the slightest interest in writing. Once Kelsi's first poem was published in the local newspaper via her classroom teacher, she was hooked. This newfound interest in writing led to more and more newspaper publications. If there were an essay contest in her class or even in her school, she would enter. She later began entering her poems for national publication and was featured several times in A Celebration of Young Poets.

For Kelsi, writing wasn't just a school project; she started keeping a journal. I recall her Aunt Henrietta gifting her with her first diary. It was the lock and key version. Somehow, this made writing more intriguing for Kelsi. Writing soon became her best subject. But, as with most writers, reading was a top priority as well.

I have often said to parents, teachers, and anyone who would listen, "once a child learns to read well, they can tackle any subject."

Henry Frank our youngest, a high school history teacher and football coach, found his strength as an orator. At a very young age, he had many opportunities to speak publicly at church and school. When he was summonsed to introduce a speaker, sometimes renowned, such as Reverend Jesse Jackson, he would first write down his introductions to rehearse them. As an orator, he started out by joining the 4-H Speech Club and would enter speech competitions in elementary school.

It didn't seem to unnerve him that several hundred spectators watched and listened to his every word. To deliver a speech with precision, you must first write it down and practice to commit it to memory.

Most of us, parents and children alike, are better at writing than we think. The key is finding a purpose for which to write.

Kelsi's purpose was to win a prize or to get published. Henry Frank's purpose for writing was to rehearse his orator delivery. My purpose for writing this parenting book is to share my knowledge and experience as a parent and parent educator as an avenue to empower other parents, teachers, grandparents, caregivers, neighbors, and others.

Parenting our two children has been my greatest passion in life. I have enjoyed every stage of the journey. This book has been on my bucket list for over 20 years. When I reflect on when I knew I would one day write this book, it is as clear as the morning sun. It was when I created the content for the parent seminars all those years ago. I knew then that I would one day convert those seminar topics into book chapters.

After 40 years in the education field, my recent retirement afforded me the time to do what I was meant to do. Write this book. It feels like putting my passion on paper. Amazing!

When asked why I want to write a book, my response is, "why must a painter paint," or "a singer sing." "It's in me, and I must share it with the world."

Unfortunately, handwriting is not one of those subjects that get a lot of attention during the school day. So how then do you expose your children to more writing?

First, become a family who reads together. When you show your love for reading, it's easier to intertwine writing and storytelling. Remind your children while reading together that someone had to write the story first, for us to enjoy reading it. Don't just say it casually; make it your mantra when reading as a family.

It's called "planting a seed." What your children hear you say often is what they will remember. As a family, write down your family history and allow everyone to contribute. Make it an ongoing fun family project. Someone will eventually take the lead as the writer.

Next, have plenty of writing materials on hand. Our children loved color, so I would purchase colorful pencils, notebooks, and index cards for summarizing stories that we read together. When the children became avid readers of chapter books, they continued to use the colorful index cards to write a summary for long chapters. These written summaries came in handy during our family book talks that I referenced in an earlier chapter.

Helping your children become good writers is not just about exposure. As parents, we must applaud their efforts. Think about it, the more they read, the better readers they will become. The same is true for writing. Good writers are developed over time.

So, what if your child's writing is not perfect? Applauding their effort will keep them motivated.

Here are a few strategies we set in motion to aide our children into becoming writers:

Occasionally, I would slip a post-it note with a simple, "I love you to the moon and back" in their lunch boxes. Then, as they grew older, I would write a letter and ask for a written response. The purpose for this was two-fold. 1. It gave me a chance to express something important to them in writing. 2. It created a purpose for them to write me back and express their feelings in writing. This can be very therapeutic.

Writing provides the time needed to formulate deeper than everyday thoughts. When you are speaking, you must say what you are going to say and move on. When you are writing, you have time to stop and ponder, erase and start over. No one knows how long it took you to get your thoughts on paper besides you.

The reader only gets to see the final product. Lucky for us as writers, they missed the many shots made in the trash can.

Kelsi and Henry Frank realized the sentiments we felt from receiving their homemade Mother's and Father's Day cards. Our reactions moved them to create more handwritten cards with elaborate drawings. I have held on to these heartfelt words for years and occasionally share with them something they have written in the past. Their expressions are priceless.

When we hold something that they shared with us in years past close to our hearts, speaks volume to a child. I am known in the family for my archives of report cards, writing samples, and standardized test results.

Henry Frank was inspired to write a book about a faraway land. I think he had an elysian brought on by his favorite author at the time, Christopher Paolini. Reading Paolini's series of books were not for the fate of heart, as they would range from 800 pages to well over 1,000.

I was aware that he was attempting to write his first book, maybe around middle school. For him, this was also the time that sports became more appealing—football in particular.

I reread what I consider a profound start of a great book a few years ago, as I cleared his room when he left home for college.

Though unfinished, I consider it a masterpiece that I will keep forever. Who knows, Henry Frank may one day wish to finish his untold story of a faraway land. But if not, I have proof to show his children, that he had the propensity for writing.

Helping our children to see the importance of being able to write doesn't have to be complicated. Once they understand the purpose, then they must care about the topic. They may need your help in finding a connection.

Start a dialogue about what appeals to them. For example, if they enjoy music, ask them to create the lyrics to a song and write it down.

Initiate a writing contest by having them write a short paper on how they would spend an extra allowance or Christmas bonus. Leave the names off and have a neutral person judge the writing for creativity and sentence structure. A dictionary may be used for spelling.

Another fun strategy we used to spark the writing potential in our children was to have everyone write a story; parents included starring "you" as a super-hero or shero. The sky is the limit when it comes to creativity. This fun family writing adventure could take several days to complete. This one was not a contest and the only criteria were the number of words of at least 100.

The writing process was introduced to our children at school and reinforced at home. As a result, most of us learned this basic process when we learned to write.

Here are the six-steps and how we reinforced them at home:

- **Step #1 Select a Topic** – In our family the example was creating a short story starring "you" as a super-hero/shero. The topic was simply super shero (Mom the Magnificent) was the name that I chose. Choosing a super-hero topic was a sure-fire winner for our children. Just in case this topic doesn't appeal to your children, try brainstorming as a family. Start by asking, "what makes them happy?" Listen carefully to their responses and make a list as they share.

Your brainstorming list may resemble this:

- Their favorite dessert
- A funny movie
- Their favorite toy
- Playing outside
- Their favorite super-hero/shero
- Family time
- Playing in the snow
- Going fishing

Read the list back to your child/children. Have them choose one thing from the list to start free-writing (writing without judgment or corrections). Encourage your young children to begin with a drawing.

Step #2 Prewriting – You may raise questions for your child to answer about the topic. Ask your child to write down the answers to your questions, as this will provide specific details to support the topic. Using the answers to these particular questions, have your child make a list or an outline. This is a good time to draw a story map. Start with a simple circle on a piece of paper. Write the main idea in the circle. Outside of the circle start listing descriptive words to describe the main idea. If super-hero is the main idea, you may see loyal, strong, warrior, fair, mammoth, colorful, etc.

Step #3 Organizing – Once all these ideas are written down, it's time to put them in order. You have heard it many times, organization is the key. I find this to be true about most things, and writing is no exception. Every good story has an interesting beginning, middle, and a strong ending. Start by organizing your facts in a logical order. What happened first? What happened second and third? These facts or events should be placed in the order of importance. You can't save the planet until you identify the problem.

Step #4 Drafting – This is when your story begins to take form. The writing is starting to look like a story. This is not the time to worry about spelling or punctuation. The difficult part is over. Allow your mind to soar with ideas that you never knew you had. Think like a detective, leaving no mystery unsolved. If you are enjoying the writing process, chances are the reader will enjoy it as well. To ensure a full-body story, make sure you have addressed who, what, when, where, why, and how. These elements are the basics of any good story.

As you can see, they don't call it the writing process for nothing. A process is something that is perfected and completed over time. Once you have practiced it several times, it becomes second nature. The good news is whether you are writing a short story or a long story, the writing process never changes.

Ok. There are only two steps left to complete:

Step #5 Revising – Ask your child to read aloud what he has written so far. This is not the time for you to correct or interrupt. When your child finishes reading, ask a few "W" questions, who, what, when, where, and so on. If your child is happy with his answers, show your enthusiasm for the story. Feel free to ask about his word choices. Remember, it is your child's story from a child's perspective.

The final step of the writing process is:

Step #6 Publishing – This simply means that the writing is ready for public viewing – AKA – the teachers, parents, or others. I kept most of our children's writings. It means a lot to them and me to see the quality of their writing at various stages of their lives.

Sharing these stories was an even bigger hit during our family time, as we shared our stories in full garb. The children would often comment, "Who knew that writing could be so much fun?"

To video record these amazing super-heroes and sheroes stories was a great way to capture how writing transformed our family time together.

We all selected a name for ourselves first. We began developing a description from head to foot. Our actions are where the depth of the story's flood gates gave way.

In 1997, the premiere of Titanic became a family affair, spearheaded by Henry Frank. We read the children's book version of the story. We purchased the toy ship and the t-shirt. Whatever memorabilia was available, he had to have it. We later purchased the movie for our home and viewed it as a family. Henry Frank was the history buff of the family. He was drawn to non-fiction at an early age. I'd like to think attending Sunday School and hearing bible stories at a young age contributed to his fascination with history. He would win the bible trivia every time and earned the nickname at our church, "the little professor." Being 6'3" now has forced them to drop the "little" part.

Photography seems to be something we all enjoyed. Even though many of our most recent pictures are stored electronically, I take great pride in my photo albums. Housed in decorative boxes, I still share these family jewels with friends and relatives.

Writing the captions for photos in our family albums didn't feel like writing to the children. Because we have a busy family, chronicling our family events with short summaries in the order of their occurrence is paramount. There is nothing worse than having hundreds of loose pictures in a box without order or captions.

When talking with your children about school, always inquire about their writing assignments. Be specific and ask to see writing samples. Your praise can set your children on a successful writing trajectory at home, at school, and in life.

So, praise the behavior and results you want to see more of, because we raise what we praise.

If you ever fall short of writing topics, here are a few to consider:

- An imaginary faraway land
- A shooting star
- A secret hide-a-way
- An alien
- The morning a parrot appeared at your door
- Your pet
- A time-capsule
- Your best friend
- Lost in the woods
- Yourself
- The best vacation ever
- What I like about school

Ask your children to add to the list. The most important thing about writing is to start. The more you write, the better writer you will become. So, focus attention on your child's persistence, not perfection.

I hope that this chapter has given you a vision for what your child can become. Children will not always be children. One day before you can exhale, your children will leave home for college or a career and maybe become a writer.

Lord, I pray our children's soul would pant for you as the deer pants for streams of water.
Psalm 42:1 KJV

Adapted by the Author

CHAPTER TEN

Helping Your Teens Succeed in Middle School, High School, and Beyond

Outcomes

In this chapter, the parent/reader will explore successful strategies for keeping middle and high schoolers focused and motivated.

"There could be no keener revelation of a society's soul than the way in which it treats its children."

Nelson Mandela – Former President of South Africa

"The greatest gifts you can give your children are the roots of responsibility and the wings of independence."

Denis Waitley – Motivational Speaker

Our children transitioning from elementary to middle school was a difficult time for both our children, Henry, and me. But this was also an exciting time for all of us. We knew that the middle school experience would come with many opportunities and challenges. Not only will our children's school environment change, but so will their social, emotional, academic, and physical well-being.

These changes are inevitable. There are no exemptions. As sure as the seasons change, all of our children will spend a portion of their lives in various life cycle stages. Generally speaking, elementary school is synonymous with children ages 6-10. Middle schoolers are adolescences who typically range from ages 11-14. High schoolers or older adolescences are usually around 15-18 of age. Of course, this is all based on birthdays and when your child starts school.

Even though the ages may vary, children will find common ground when they reach middle school. As a life-long educator, my teaching career started out teaching third and fourth-grade students. After a short while, I matriculated to teaching middle schoolers, putting my K-8 Reading Certification to good use. This was my first introduction to technology in the classroom. I considered being a Computer Reading Lab Instructor, my ideal teaching assignment, except for the salary.

Using my first-hand knowledge about students who transition from elementary to middle school, I shared insights with my children, who are four years apart.

Few parents realize that middle school is when many children lose interest in school altogether. The loss of interest makes this transition a critical turning point in our children's education. Their success in middle school will determine their success in high school, college, career, and life.

As our children prepare to enter middle school, we need to know that our support not only matters, it is necessary.

We all know that fear is derived from the unknown; that being said, we can reduce our children's fear and anxiety by providing them with information, guidance, love, and understanding.

When our children's elementary school years were coming to an end, their fifth-grade teacher sent home a packet about what to expect from middle school. As a family, we reviewed this information together after dinner over ice cream. It's small gestures like ice cream that can make a stressful situation more relaxed.

The information that we received from their soon-to-be middle school was also invaluable. There were many user-friendly tidbits included, putting the children and us as parents at ease. We received dates and times to meet our children's new teachers, principals, counselors, and other staff members. One of the best ways to acclimate your child to middle school is to include your child on the initial school visit.

Learning the school's physical layout together was helpful, as I was able to point out interesting aspects of the building that my children may not have noticed. I remember their excitement over finding their locker location, something they never had in elementary school. It was good for their teachers to put a student's face with that of a parent. No one ever said that favor was fair. I know first-hand the acceptance a student receives when the teacher has a connection with the parent. It's called human nature. As a mother, I never missed the opportunity to conference with my children's teachers. I always had questions to ask the teacher. If they would say something like, "Your child is a good student." I would ask them, "what makes my child a good student?" With a smile, of course.

Many parents make the mistake of becoming less involved in their children's lives both in and out of school as they become older. Unfortunately, when you stop and think about it, our children are faced with more distractions that can get them off course as they become older than in elementary school.

So why is it that parents show up for every event to support their children in elementary school and not middle school? I have witnessed the parental support as it dissipated in middle school. Even as a middle school teacher in Arkansas in the mid '80s, I found myself taking students home who were not picked up after a school-sponsored event.

As I would escort their child to the front door, the parents were always so gracious and would sometimes invite me in for dinner. I always graciously declined.

So what makes middle school so dissimilar from elementary school from a parent's perspective?

Here are a few things to consider:

- As a parent, you formed a close relationship with your child's teacher, who taught the four core subjects.
- As a parent, you understood how the curriculum was structured: Reading and math were taught before lunch, then science and social studies in the afternoon. We all remember that notorious spelling test every Friday.

- Students had fewer extracurricular activities that were offered after-school.
- As a parent, you knew what time to expect your child at home, because they either walked to school, rode the bus, or you transported them to and from school.
- As a parent, you understood the homework rules and could access them from the homework hotline portal if needed. These assignments were sent electronically by one teacher for all subjects.
- As a parent, you understood that all levels of coursework were the same, as there were not advance classes to choose from within the classroom.
- As a parent, you knew where your child's class was located in case of an emergency.
- As a parent, you knew who your kid's friends were and their parents via school activities or birthday parties.
- As a parent, you could volunteer to chaperone all school or class field trips.
- As a parent, you knew how to contact your child's teacher or counselor.

In contrast – In middle school, from a parent's perspective.

Here are a few things to consider:

- As a parent, you may have difficulty connecting with all of your child's teachers. There is a different teacher for each subject. There are more subjects now, including a few electives.
- As a parent, you are trying to understand how the multidimensional curriculum is designed. Who gets to take Pre-Algebra vs. Algebra?
- As a parent, you may struggle to keep up with the inconsistency of test dates. No more Friday spelling tests.
- As a parent, you must arrange to pick up your child from after-school band rehearsal, football practice, or another extracurricular activity that meets after school.
- As a parent, you must decide if your child is responsible enough to become a latch-key kid.
- As a parent, you must learn to access the electronic homework hotline portal for several teachers, not only homework assignment but general announcements and school closings. Thank goodness for the agenda books and planners that were introduced in middle school.
- As a parent, we had to educate ourselves on which courses were advanced and the prerequisites.
- As a parent, locating your child's room during an emergency may be difficult since your child

will be in a different classroom for each subject.

- As a parent, it is more challenging to know who your children's friends are. It is not unusual for your children to have a study buddy or just a buddy in each class. Their circle of friends has grown, and because many parents are not as involved as they were in elementary school, you may not get acquainted with them all.
- As a parent, there are fewer field trips to chaperone, which is where I connected with many of the other parents.
- As a parent of a middle schooler, you have an entire team of teachers to become acquainted with.
- This does not include the school administration or the extracurricular activity leaders.

None of these dissimilarities are bad; however, they can be frustrating if you are caught off guard. So be informed and be proactive. Start by talking to your children about any concerns they may have about starting middle school. Then, be keenly aware of the changes your children are experiencing socially, emotionally, academically, and physically.

Reassure them that these changes are normal and

every child who transitions from elementary to middle school experiences these growing pains.

Don't just focus on the challenges of the transition.

Ask your child, "what are you excited about starting middle school?" Be ready to listen when your child is ready to speak. Give them your full attention when they want you just to listen. As a parent, you can be your child's most significant influencer. Remind your child that this is a time of more independence. They will be making decisions about which clubs or sports they may be interested in.

As a middle schooler, it will be more critical than ever for your child to get organized. An agenda book or academic planner is an excellent investment to track assignments and tests. Color-coded notebooks are a great way to differentiate one subject from the other. Setting up a study routine with a consistent time and space to complete homework assignments daily will reduce stress for you and your child.

Our rule of thumb was that there would be a mommade homework assignment if there is no teacher homework assignment. I cannot stress enough the importance of acclimating our children to the rigor of daily homework. In our household, homework was a given, Monday – Friday. This schedule allowed us to spend family time during the weekends. Many of these weekends we spent traveling to Arkansas, which was a priority to acquaint the children with my side of the family.

Our children understood that homework was an

extension of what was learned at school that day. Even when they completed their homework assignments at school or during their after-school care program, reading was considered homework.

Why is it essential to build good study habits in our children at a young age? When our children become accustomed to studying outside of the school day, they are more likely to tackle the demands of advanced coursework in high school and college.

Building stamina for reading and studying is much like building stamina in the gym. When you start lifting weights in the gym, you may start at 20lbs and two repartitions. The more you lift, you are building muscle and stamina to go heavier and longer. Before long, you can lift 30lbs with more reps.

Are your children intimidated by the size of a big book? Throughout my career, parents would share how their children or grandchildren shied away from a big book. Before middle school, your child should be reading chapter books, which are generally bigger and take longer to finish. Don't forget the index cards for summarizing each chapter.

Praising your child for reading more extensive books will help build confidence. Remember, we raise what we praise. If you want to see more effort, keep the praises coming. Teach them to ask for help when they need it. Please share examples of how you have to ask for help when you need it at work. Let them know that no one knows everything, and we all need help sometimes. If you cannot give your child the needed help, reach out to your child's teacher. Try exchanging contact information with a few of the parents. It's good to have someone to brainstorm with who is in a similar situation.

Getting to know the parents is an excellent way to get to know your child's friends. Teach your child what to look for in a friend. Do they respect themselves and others? Do they use good judgment? Do they respect authority? Do they have a positive outlook on life?

Let your child know that you support his new school and plan to be involved. Encourage his involvement in extracurricular activities. Some kids can't wait to get involved, while others need that pep talk.

Start by sharing the benefits of being involved.

- You will learn new things.
- You will make new friends with similar interests.
- You will learn to be a leader.
- You will enjoy school more.
- You will get to find out what you are good at.
- You will get to relieve stress and have fun.

Just like in elementary school, a reasonable bed time is imperative for success in middle school. It will take a well-rested and well-fed individual to excel in middle school. The days seem longer with the changing of classes each period. Many clubs and sports will take place after-school, and then there is homework.

TV was a luxury during the week and was limited to one of their favorite shows each. There were no TVs in their bedrooms, so they had to compromise and take turns watching the family TV in the family room.

Henry and I worked full-time, so when the children wanted to sleep a little longer on the weekend, we welcomed it.

As parents, we know that middle school is the stepping stone for high school. Many of the changes your children manage in middle school are the same ones they will experience in high school, just bigger. Chances are the new high school will be bigger and better. During high school, they will continue to grow physically, mentally, emotionally, and socially. High school is where our children truly become young adults. How our children handle high school will teach us a lot about how they will take on life. They will have more responsibilities and more options, not to mention more independence. Our children will be responsible for setting up their schedules and getting to those scheduled classes on time in high school. This new school will have new rules that may challenge your child's maturity level. They may start to feel all grown up, but they still must learn to follow the rules.

Unlike middle school, in high school, our children will decide which classes to take. It is important for them to have some idea of their future, like attending college, starting a career, or attending trade school. The classes they take will set them on a college or technical pathway.

Many of the same decisions they made in middle school must be made in high school, such as how to manage time and whether they will participate in extracurricular activities. Often, who you will ultimately become as a person is shaped during team sports, holding an office like Student Government President, Marching Band member, Bridge Builders, Chess Club, Book Club, School Newspaper, or Yearbook Staff.

It's vital in high school to regularly meet with your assigned counselor to ensure that the classes you sign-up for match your future plans.

Advanced Placement (AP) classes are a good idea if you plan to attend a college or university. Some colleges/universities will give credit for specific AP courses. These classes could result in you saving time and dollars during your college years.

The classes you choose should also match your area of interest. For example, if you want to become a doctor, you may want to consider science, math, biology, or chemistry classes. Again, your high school counselor is your best resource when matching your interest with your coursework.

Either way, our children should take full advantage to learn as much in high school as possible. Knowledge is indeed power, whether you choose to go to college or start a career.

As a parent, you can encourage your child to select classes that complement their personality. Sometimes our children may not acknowledge their strength in a particular area. Instead, we can remind them of a time when they excelled and enjoyed it.

Unless the school Counselor recommends your child take study hall, don't waste your time. This slot could be filled with taking a drawing or music class, which could very well become their favorite class.

I have never had a student tell me that study hall was their favorite class. It takes a solid disciplinarian to get students to study during study hall. When I walk down the school hallway, I can usually identify the study hall class immediately. It's a class where there is no studying taking place. Seriously.

Electives are options that are not broadly offered in middle school. Adversely, in high school, there are more classes offered, there are many electives to choose from as well. These are classes that you elect to take outside of what is required for each grade level.

Having electives is an opportunity for your children to take classes that can help them discover their talents, like the band, choir, drama, writing, computer, etc. Don't be surprised if these classes are their favorites.

Encourage your children to join clubs or organizations with an emphasis on community service projects. These types of experiences will help them build character and distract them from becoming self-centered. People who give their time and service to others tend to find more enjoyment in life.

High school is also a time for more standardized testing. Will my child take the ACT or SAT? If your child is college-bound, this should be investigated based on the school's (college/university) requirements. There is also the (EOC) End of Course exams to consider. These subject-based exams will count as a percent of their overall grade.

Grades are certainly more important in high school than in middle school. This is when your (GPA) Grade Point Average starts to count. The higher your grades, the higher your GPA. Good grades will not only affect your college acceptance, but many employers will consider your GPA for job placement.

High school is a time for more independence. Learning how to handle peer pressure is part of growing up. The close relationship that you have established with your child over the years will definitely come in handy. As a parent, we must trust that what we have taught our children about valuing themselves, honesty, respect for others, etc. will be remembered and matters.

Stay connected with your high schooler with open communication daily. Remind them that with additional freedom comes additional responsibility. Be honest with your children about mistakes you have made and survived. When your children see you as perfect, they are less likely to share their missteps with you. Let your children know that they are not alone. There is a wealth of resources via the high school to help them with any situation.

Please encourage your child to get to know their high school counselor, teachers, librarian, advisors, and other school personnel. Many high schools have a Student Assistance Program to assist with issues that may be out of your realm of expertise.

I would always share the importance of school with my children and how elementary school prepares you for middle school and middle school for high school. Seize the moment by taking advantage of every opportunity to learn and grow. This is your "say so" in the quality of life you will create for your future.

It all starts here!

Father, I pray my children would ask and that you would generously give wisdom to them as you promise.
James 1:5 KJV

Adapted by the Author

CHAPTER ELEVEN

Positive Disciplinarians: Setting Limits for our Children

Outcomes

In this chapter, the parent/reader will explore the benefits and consequences of setting limits for children.

"We raise what we praise."

Brenda Reed Pilcher – Mother, Entrepreneur, Life-Long Educator and Author

"I think of discipline as the continual everyday process of helping a child learn self-discipline."

Fred Rogers – American Celebrity, Mr. Roger's Neighborhood

Why is "Positive Discipline" necessary? Positive discipline promotes and encourages the development of life skills and wholesome and healthy relationships in the family, school, work, play, and community.

Without it, there would be no society in which we can thrive. Without the knowledge of positive discipline, parents and children would find themselves living in chaos.

As a child, I was raised in an environment of love and discipline. So as a mother raising our children in an atmosphere of love and discipline came naturally to me. I knew innately without love, there is no discipline, and without discipline, there is no love. This is not to say that when parents don't discipline their children, they don't love them, but it is to say when we learn better, we should do better. I have repeated this several times in this book, "knowledge is power."

One of the most difficult parental challenges we face is discipline. So, where do we start?

This is not a chapter about whether to spank or not to spank. Instead, my goal is to share some insights to get you thinking about the path you and your children will take when it comes to discipline.

As a parent, you are in total control and will steer the wheel positively or negatively when it comes to disciplining your children.

It is important to note that discipline is a journey that affects the entire family. Sometimes just stopping and thinking can make us a more positive disciplinarian. Many of our adverse reactions are birthed out of reacting too quickly.

At a very early age, children must learn the difference between right and wrong. Toddlers can differentiate between yes and no. Once the rules are established, reinforcing the rules consistently is paramount for successful results. Rules that are not reinforced are like having no rules at all.

Raising a well-rounded child will help to make things easier for you as a positive disciplinarian. When we help our children develop both socially and emotionally, they will respect us as authority figures and get along better with others.

Good discipline requires self-control and confidence. Creating a home environment that fosters curiosity about learning will make a huge difference. Children must also learn how to play and cooperate with other children. Whether your child attends daycare or you are a stay-at-home parent, you must model what sharing looks like. Take the time to model for your child how to take turns when playing with you, their siblings, and with other children.

When reading together, have your child respond to the character's feelings. Let your child know what makes you happy or sad about the story. Discuss why. When children get their "Why" questions answered, they grow to be more curious, which leads to more learning.

When I was a classroom teacher, many of my discipline incidents were derived from children who were not good in school in general and reading in particular. So, imagine the frustration felt by children when they are struggling academically in school.

I have always known that partnering with my students' parents was the only way I could help my students become better readers. The more the parent read with their child at home, the easier my job was at school. Everyone wins when we all contribute to children's success.

Once you can show them their progress and build their confidence for learning, the discipline dissipates. Not only did the student's behavior improve at school, but also at home. When we reward the behavior we want to see more of with praise, we will see better behavior. We raise what we praise has been my mantra for more than four decades. It works.

I have examples of the positive effects of praise with my children, as well as the many children that crossed my path in schools, church, my extended family, sorority, and my community. I am my child's first teacher, my home is my child's first school, and praise is my child's first love language.

Never underestimate the power of praise. Praise can change the trajectory of a child's life. It can turn a child who feels defeated into a child who has confidence in himself. Praise can cause a bowed down head to look to the stars. It shows your child what you think about him or her and their ability. It means the world to a child to know that we recognize them and not just their accomplishments. When we praise our children, we must aim our praise toward the child and not their accomplishments. There is a difference between saying, "I am proud of you for winning your race vs. I am proud of you for never giving up; you have what it takes."

Praise can be that little boost that your child needs to go from good to great. Of course, praise is received differently by different children. But whether it shows or not, they all need it. Some children may not express it openly, but it changes who they are from the inside.

Working with children and youth throughout my career, I could always sense a child who lacked praise at home. I made it my mission to feel their tanks while they were in my care. There is a difference between praise, and authentic praise, and children can decipher the difference. As an educator, I learned early in my career that praise must be specific to be believable. Instead of saying, "you are good in math", try saying," as a third grader you have mastered your multiplication facts early. You are ahead of the game." See the difference?

In the words of Fred Rogers – Mr. Roger's Neighborhood, the goal of disciplining a child is to teach them self-discipline over time. Self-discipline is something we all need, and even adults wish they had more of it. With self-discipline, there is nothing you can't achieve. If there is something we want to become better at, we can accomplish the goal with more self-discipline, time, and effort.

We have already established that discipline is one of the most difficult parental challenges. It takes time, effort, knowledge, and most importantly, love. When we love our children we want what is best for them. It helped me as a parent when our children were younger to know that all parents struggle with disciplining their children.

Ultimately, it is the lessons our children learn from their mistakes that make the discipline so rewarding. Therefore, we must teach our children to have a positive attitude about mistakes. Let them know that we all make them.

Consider the relationship you have with your children.

Here are a few questions to ponder:

Do you spend quality time together?

Do you follow through with your promises?

Do you show them love and affection?

When you need to punish them, does the punishment match the behavior?

Are you setting reasonable expectations for your children?

Do you model good self-discipline?

Our children will mimic what they see us do. We can't always be running late and expect our children to learn to be on time. We can't stay up all night and expect them to honor their bedtime. We cannot be a sore loser and expect our children to be a good sport.

Having children has made me a better person in many ways. First, I was fully aware of the eyes and ears that followed me around. Second, I will never forget how they were mortified by a visiting family member who used a discolorful word that begins with "s."

They ran to me to deliver the news and still talk about the indiscretion to this day. I think the person saying it surprised them more than the word itself.

As a parent of two children, I know firsthand that discipline is just as individualistic as learning. Every child is uniquely wired. What works for one may not work for the other.

All children want to be disciplined with rules and a structured environment. Having a routine is a form of discipline. For example, knowing what time is dinner time and bedtime make a child feel loved and secure. Not knowing and not having structure in the home have an adverse effect on your children.

Set realistic rules and consequences. Discuss and explain the rules and consequences calmly. Repeat the rules often and explain how making a mistake is not the end of the world. Teach your children the importance of learning from their mistakes. It's how we grow better and wiser. Cite a few of your missteps to encourage your children to keep improving and moving forward.

All children are unique in how they learn, respond to praise, and respond to discipline. Here are a few things that I know for sure that all children need when it comes to discipline: Discipline must be respectful. When explaining the rules, be firm, but avoid arguments. Patience will come in handy, as it may take your child a week or so to internalize the rules and know that you mean business. Teach and model mutual respect. Positive discipline should be effective long-term. The more they understand the discipline expectations, the better the outcome. Take the time for training. Ask, "what is your understanding of these rules?" Show your children how these rules are designed to keep them safe and help them to grow into responsible members of the family and society. Please share some of the rules that you must follow and how they benefit you, the family, and society.

The more they know, the better your discipline expectations will go.

Here are a few positive discipline suggestions to keep in mind:

- Please help your child feel encouraged by praising their effort, as well as their achievements.
- Set clear rules. Make sure the rules are age-appropriate.
- Be consistent. It's easy to put off a punishment when you are tired.
- Praise good behavior. We raise what we praise.
- Don't overreact when your child breaks a rule. Turn this into a teachable moment with encouragement.
- Have family meetings to solve problems with cooperation and mutual respect.
- Give children meaningful chores to teach them to contribute to the family's success.
- Use proper timing for punishment to improve your effectiveness.
- Use positive "Time Out."
- Teach your children that mistakes are opportunities to learn and grow.
- Focus on the solution instead of the consequences.
- Make sure you leave your child feeling cared for and respected.
- Have fun with your children. They are less likely to misbehave when they are happy with themselves.

Thus far, this chapter has focused mainly on positive

discipline. So, where does punishment fit in?

I recall only one spanking during my childhood. The rule was to come home directly from school and change into my play clothes. I walked to and from school with children from my neighborhood, but I also had friends who lived beyond where I lived. It was third grade when I decided that I would go beyond my house and walk my best friend at the time home. She was not required to change out of her school clothes, so we decided to play a quick game of kickball with some kids in her neighborhood. What started out as a quick game ended up as a full-on tournament. I was having so much fun. I lost track of time. When I finally arrived home at least an hour later, my mother was standing in the back yard with a switch in her hand. The rest, as they say, is history. Needless to say, after that, I was the first one home after school before any of my siblings.

The positive discipline that I have written about so far is a process that is perfected overtime with patience, love, and encouragement.

I prefer to use a form of punishment that will have a lasting effect. This may require withholding a reward or privilege for a period of time. I always tried to give my children a warning prior to administering punishment. They were never surprised and had ample time to correct their behavior. The difference between punishment and discipline is a powerful child – Danny Silk.

Putting off a punishment never works. This is why a punishment should follow immediately after the offense.

We must help our children understand clearly the connection between misbehavior and punishment.

Remember, the end goal is to teach our children self-discipline. Use real-world examples of the consequences that were applied due to a lack of discipline. Unfortunately, there are many instances in our society and pop culture that you can reference.

The big picture is that discipline hinges on the relationship you have with your children. The key to discipline is building relationships. Building relationships is the cornerstone of everything. It will determine how successful our children will be in our family, at school, with friends, and in society.

I believe how we discipline our children at home will reflect how successful they will be in life.

Discipline teaches us how to be and how to become. It is easier for us to learn than it is to unlearn and then relearn. Once you learn something you have it. Embrace it the first time. We often make life more difficult than it has to be. Discipline is everything, it helps us to become who God intended for us to be.

Dare to discipline.

Father, I pray our children have what you promised; no fear, power, love and self-discipline.
2 Timothy 1:7 KJV

Adapted by the Author

CHAPTER TWELVE

Study Secrets of a Good Student

Outcomes

In this chapter, the parent/reader will examine the characteristics of a successful student and strategies to help them manage their learning.

"Good or bad, what we do often is what we do well."
Brenda Reed Pilcher – Mother, Entrepreneur, Life-long Educator and Author

"Spend time with those you love. One of these days, you will say either, I wish I had, or I am glad I did. "
Zig Ziglar – American Author, Salesman, and Motivational Speaker

In this chapter, we will unpack various study secrets that lead to successful experiences in school and ultimately in life.

To most students, the word "study" has a negative connotation. As a parent, we must illustrate for our children that studying is simply "learning." We all are learning something new every day and not just in school. Studying doesn't have to be dull or lonesome. It can be interesting and communicative. A more significant part of studying is attitude. When we approach any activity with a positive attitude, including studying, we get more out of it.

When we replace the term studying with learning, it will help our children see that this is something that we engage in every day. Anything that we do carefully requires learning or studying. For example, when you go to a restaurant that you have never been to before, you study the menu. When you open the box of a new game or toy, you must review the instructions. When you plan an outdoor activity, you must study the weather.

Studying is important because it teaches us what we need to know and why we need to know it. Learning something new is one of the great pleasures of life. It helps us to grow more and think more extensively.

Ask your child the age-old question, "what do you want to be when you grow up?" Whatever answer they give, remind them that they must learn how to do it first in order for them to become that. When we study, we learn and when we learn, we study.

Teaching our children to think positively about things that other children may not see as positive may not be easy, but it is necessary.

I tried to convey the importance of studying and testing in a positive light to my children. I refused to be the kind of parent that complained to my children about the volume of school work assigned by the teacher. If I could not get them to see the positive aspects of studying and learning, my job as a parent would be an uphill battle.

I made it my mission to paint the picture of those who have and those who have not is correlated to how much they study and learn. I told our children stories about how studying can get them into college free of charge. Studying can make a difference between a professional career and manual labor.

I scored a few points when I explained to our children that everything that they already know, they once had to learn to do it. They got it!

Our children knew that studying at home was not just limited to what was learned at school. Homework was a priority because we were a family of learners. We would research a vocabulary word that was introduced while we read together. We would read and study topics that were not easy to discuss, like death and divorce.

Studying is one of those things that makes your child more competitive. When their peers may be watching TV or playing video games after school, those who spend time studying at home build stamina for more challenging work ahead.

One of my favorite quotes that I repeated in every teacher/parent seminar is, "What we do often is what we do well." It's true, good or bad, constructive or destructive. We become the thing we spend most of our time doing. I was keenly aware of this, so as a mother, I tried to fill my time with activities that would engage me, enlighten me, empower me, and educate me. I knew that for us to raise positive, happy, and well-rounded children, we had to be all of these things as well. We cannot control everything in life, but there are many things that we can control.

Positive thinking is a choice. If you want to be smart, you can be. If you think you can do something, you can. Everything we do or have done started with a thought. Teach your children to have a "can do" attitude. Model this attitude in your home. Our children will be more like us than unlike us.

Just like everything else, our children may have different ways they study best. For example, one may study best immediately afterschool. Some children may require some downtime to regroup before beginning their homework.

Our children were allowed to have a light snack before homework and dinner. What they chose was not of great concern because our pantry rarely housed unhealthy snacks. Fruits, graham crackers with apple sauce, or yogurt were our "go-to" snacks. Their candy intake was usually inside of a movie theater.

Like us, our children have a body rhythm. Observe your children and help them to identify what time and how they study best. Even though our children had a study desk and chair in their bedrooms, finding one sprawled out on their bedroom floor was not unusual.

Playing soft music during study time may work for one and not the other. Our children were fortunate to have their bedrooms for studying to adopt a system that worked for them. After individual study time, some of our best family study times were outside on a blanket under a tree in our backyard or on the trampoline.

One of our house rules was to minimize distraction during study time. That meant no phone calls, TV, radio, or visitors. When you have rules for the important stuff, your children will grow up valuing those same things.

I named this chapter Study Secrets of a Good Student, not that it's really a secret, but rather to show that when we unveil what makes a good student, we can ensure that our children know what it takes to excel in school and ultimately in life. Excellence is not an accident. It's the result of working smart, not hard, with organization and purpose. Once you establish a few of these routines, they will become second nature for your children.

There are a few things that I know for sure, but this is one thing that I surely know. And that is…we all make time for the things that are important to us. I would always tell the children to complete their "have to" list to spend time on their "want to' list. But, this philosophy wasn't just for them. I use it in my own life.

As an education consultant responsible for training teachers and parents alike, I was constantly studying and learning. Highlighters and index cards were always in high demand in our home. I used them to prepare for my presentations and I taught our children to do the same.

I would highlight what was important, then transcribe the highlighted material onto the index cards. When I was finished studying, I would review my index cards leading up to my presentation. The children still use index cards for chapter book summaries.

Even though I have retired from my consulting work, I still use index cards to jot down questions and comments for my book club discussions. Good habits die hard.

Scheduling study time is key to your child's success. It's not something that we do if we have time, scheduling study time is a must. This is the only way that we can ensure that the critical projects were completed. Just like us, our children must learn to multi-task. When there is homework, a test, or a project due for multiple subjects, a chunk of time must be allotted for each task. These tasks are forever evolving, which means our children must learn to pivot on-demand.

A helpful strategy that I encouraged was to complete the most difficult task first. If math is more of a challenge than spelling, complete the math portion first.

Why do some children accomplish more in the same amount of time than others? They have simply learned to use their time more efficiently. When possible, starting homework assignments before the end of school is a wise use of time. Sometimes teachers allow students "study time" in class when assignments are completed. This will give your child more time to engage in a fun activity of their choosing.

Discuss with your child the types of assignments that can be done in transit. As an active family, we took advantage of the back seat of our vehicle to house books. Children's audiobooks were among their favorites were for longer excursions. Studying spelling words or math facts were the perfect assignments for shorter trips to football or band practices.

Having discussions about their school day was my favorite car ride topic. There were no distractions of the home to divert their attention from my open-ended inquiries.

Here are a few of my favorites:

- What did you learn at school today?
- What happened today that made you laugh?
- What did you not like about school today?
- Did anyone get in trouble today?
- Who did you play with today?
- Did you learn anything new today?
- Tell me something the teacher said to you today?

These are a series of questions that I loved asking the children. Not all at once and in no particular order. Asking these questions wasn't just for my benefit. They also served as a release for the children. They could get it all out, the good and the bad.

This was their confirmation that I truly cared about how they spent their day. It was an exchange of information, as they wanted me to share how my day went as well. I didn't sugar coat it. When I had a bad day, I would share it. Children need to know that every day will not be perfect. After sharing what a horrible day I had, I would always interject, I am sure tomorrow will be better.

This was my opportunity to talk about "attitudes" and how I can control how I react to any situation.

I loved getting their feedback to these questions. I learned so much about their personalities, likes, and dislikes. Some of my questions were designed to let them know that it's ok not to have a good day every day or enjoy every single activity. There were aspects of my job that I enjoyed more than others. It's all a part of life and knowing who you are and what makes you happy or fulfilled.

Finding out who got in trouble sheds light on their behavior in class as well as their peers. Most children are honest to a fault, especially at a young age. That's why these discussions are so powerful. They will also set the stage for more serious discussions as they grow older. If the same child's name is associated with getting in trouble consistently, this could open the door to a dialogue about who to choose as a friend.

Finding out what new learning they experienced each day lets me know if they were being challenged. If they never learned anything new, I would be concerned about their overall school experience.

The last on the list was my favorite question to ask the children. "Tell me something your teacher said to you today?" This gave me insight into their relationship with their teachers. It also informed me if the teacher was an encourager. Does she or he make an effort to communicate with all the students? Does she or he like their job or children in particular?

As you can see, the secrets of a good student has a lot to do with the role that you play in your child's education. Many of these things must be set in motion by you, the parent. As your children become older, all that you have taught them will become second nature.

Once your children understand the importance of studying and learning and have a routine in place, next comes organizational skills. None of this will work without a system of organization. It is pretty simple and will stick with your children throughout their lives. It all starts with planning ahead.

I cannot think of a time in my life when being organized wasn't important. Parents need to know that organization is a skill that must be learned. Once it's learned, it must be practiced until it becomes a part of your child's routine.

Why is being organized so important? Being organized will allow what you know and will learn to work in your favor. It does no good to complete a homework assignment if you cannot find it to get it turned in on time.

Having a place to put completed assignments is just as important as completing the assignment. Deciding what to wear to school each day should not cause your child to be late for school. As children, my five siblings and I were required to lay out our school clothes the night before bedtime. If there was any ironing to be done, the night before school was the time to do it.

These became non-negotiables for our children. Returning completed homework assignments to their backpacks and laying out school clothes the night before allowed us to start our day stress-free.

Time is one of the "secrets" of a good student. How their time is organized is just as important. Being organized will help them to accomplish their schoolwork, which leaves more time for fun activities.

Two factors will help make time and organization work for your children. First, setting goals (to-do lists) and second, having a schedule. A goal can be small at first and should be age-appropriate. Scheduling a chunk of time for each task will keep things moving in the right direction. These chunks of time should be flexible, as every assignment is different.

I would be remiss if I didn't share a few study skills that every successful student should know.

For more success in reading:

- Have books available in your home on topics that your children are interested in.
- Read together as a family.
- Use index cards to list new vocabulary words. Write the definition on the back.
- Use the index cards as a word game later.
- Before reading preview the chapter. Pay attention to headings, large and bold type.

Read chapter summaries.

- Summarize chapters on index cards.
- Read ahead of the teacher's assignment.
- Read and re-read for better comprehension.

For more success in math:

- Learn your math facts from memory.
- Practice solving word problems. Make a game of it. Ask your children a random word problem while driving them to practice or the grocery store.
- Allow your children to weigh and estimate the cost of produce.
- Have a calculator on hand at the grocery store. Have your children add up the cost while you shop.

For more success in spelling:

- Always write down your spelling words. Seeing and writing spelling words will help you to remember how to spell them.
- Practice spelling words while riding in the car.
- Give your child a spelling pre-test. Have them write down the ones that they missed. Give them another pre-test. Start early in the week in case more practice is needed.

- Write spelling words on index cards. Use these cards as a word game later.

I have written entire chapters on strategies and tips to help your child improve in reading, math, and writing. If we can get our children off to a good start in these three subject areas, all other learning will take care of itself. We must help our children create a learning and studying mindset. The key is to make learning fun and engaging.

Why is it that some children believe that they can tackle anything that they put their minds to? This learning mindset has been instilled in them already. It's not too late to instill it in your children as well. If we only allow them to try things they are already good at, they will never grow. Building a learning mindset means to try something new or try it in a new way. It takes a level of discomfort to grow. It's the fear of the unknown. All of those unanswered questions can be stifling.

Ask anyone who has stepped outside of their comfort zone to learn something new about their experience. The results out-weigh the discomfort ten-fold.

Remind your children that you are in this "learning thing" together. They don't have to do it alone. If your child is not already hooked on learning, the strategies and information in this chapter can be a game-changer.

If you don't give up on them, they will not give up on themselves.

. . .

God, please cultivate in our children the ability to show true humility toward everyone.

Titus 3:2 KJV

Adapted by the Author

CHAPTER THIRTEEN

How to Raise a Good Listener

Outcomes

In this chapter, the parent/reader will identify what it means to be a good listener and explore strategies to improve parent and child communication.

"All the love in the world cannot make up the lack of leadership in a child's life."
John Rosemond – American columnist, public speaker, and Author on Parenting

"The word LISTEN contains the same letters as the word SILENT."
Alfred Brendel – Austrian Classical Pianist, Poet, Author

"The biggest communication problem is we do not listen to understand; we listen to reply."
Stephen Covey – American Educator, Author, Businessman and Keynote Speaker

Do you consider yourself to be a "good listener?"
What is required to be a "good listener?"
Are we born to be good at listening?"

How can you help your child become better at listening?

What can you do as a parent to become a better listener?

These are just a few of the questions that I will attempt to answer in this chapter.

My interest in "listening" dates back to my Thesis as a graduate student at the University of Nebraska at Omaha. This topic was in high demand among classroom teachers and parents alike. I have experience in both arenas, so when I tell you that little has changed since my grad school thesis, trust me.

From a teacher's perspective, listening well and following directions are two of the most significant skills to learn for student success in school.

Did you know that students spend more time listening than they do reading, writing, or speaking?

Listening and following directions go hand in hand. You can't do one well without the other. Listening is more than just hearing because you can hear something and clearly not understand it. Your response to listening with understanding may be completely different from what you heard.

Have you ever watched a movie with your spouse or a friend? They asked you a question about a scene and you didn't know how to respond. This is a perfect example of the difference between hearing and listening. You sat and watched the movie, but you were not listening. Therefore, there was little or no understanding.

Listening and following directions are skills, and like most skills, they must be taught. Once they are taught, they must be practiced over and over again.

Without these two essential skills, the classroom can be a struggle for students. In elementary school, children spend approximately 50% of their time listening to the teacher. This makes it critical that they become proficient at listening. The percent of time spent listening increases in high school and college.

Of all the communication skills like reading, writing, and speaking, listening is used the most often.

Dick Lee and Delmar Hatesohl – Extension and Agricultural Information – University of Missouri cited the following: 70 – 80 percent of our waking hours are spent in some form of communication. Of that time, we spend 9 percent writing, 16 percent reading, 30 percent speaking, and 45 percent listening. Unfortunately, this study also confirmed that most of us are poor and inefficient listeners.

How many times have you told your children that they don't listen? How many times have your children said to you that you don't listen?

What is required to be a good listener?

1. Concentration
2. Understanding and
3. Appropriate Response

Concentration – focus on what is being said

without distractions. Learning to pay attention is the first step to learning to be a good listener. As a parent, when you teach your child to pay attention at home, they will do better at paying attention at school.

Here are several things that parents can do at home to encourage better listening skills:

- Participate in daily conversations with your children. When you engage them in conversations that they care about, they will pay attention as you speak. Don't forget to ask questions.
- Reading to and with your children gives them practice in paying attention. Don't forget to ask questions.
- Sharing stories about our childhood was always an attention grabber for our children.
- Play games that require your children to pay attention and follow directions. "Simon Says" was our favorite.
- Any type of matching or word game that necessitated listening, memory, paying attention, and following directions gave our children the practice they needed and was fun at the same time.
- Maintain eye contact is a listening skill that we never out-grow. Teaching this one to our children was necessary for multiple

rationalities. There is something about looking a person in the eye that commands attention.

- As a classroom teacher, I would walk over and touch the shoulder of a student that wasn't listening. I tried not to stop teaching to get one student's attention. This strategy worked at home as well.

- Ask your child to repeat what you said. This works well with the important stuff.

- Don't give instructions from another room of your home. Let your child know that you have something to say, make eye contact first, then say it.

- Give your child the same respect when they are talking to you. Stop what you are doing and listen.

- Try not to interrupt your child's playtime to get the point across unless it's imperative.

Understanding – comprehending what is being said. There are many things that parents can do at home to encourage listening comprehension.

- Talk to your child to increase their vocabulary. The larger their vocabulary, the better their understanding.

- Be specific and use descriptive words during conversations.

- Introduce unusual words while talking. Ask your child, "what is your understanding of the unusual word that I just used?"
- When interacting with your child, do more asking than telling.
- When reading with your child, ask them to retell parts of the story.

What is the moral of the story?
What conclusions can you draw?
What was your favorite part?
How would you change the ending?

- Talking to your children while doing the household chores can provide the needed distraction your child needs.
- Make the conversation about them and not the chore itself.
- Talk about yourself to your children. The more they know about you, the more connected to you they will feel. Our childhood stories were our children's favorite.
- Discuss audiobooks while riding in the car together. Ask the who, what, when, where, why, and how questions.

In my classroom, I could always identify those students whose parents talked to them at home. They were the most inquisitive and had a richer vocabulary. I enjoyed interacting with young people, whether it was my children or my students. I could always gauge their intellectual progress by their verbal interaction.

When I was in the presence of children, it was my mission to build their self-esteem. Helping a child see their worth, is worth its weight in gold. Priceless.

There is no age limit for self-esteem building. We all need it at every stage of our lives.

You can start by saying things like this to your children:

- That's an interesting thought!
- You were wise to think of that!
- That makes a lot of sense!
- You are full of information!
- Thanks for helping me to understand that better!

You have "healing hands," is what I would say to Henry Frank when he would reach up to rub my head or back, which ever one I'd indicate was ailing me. He was not tall enough to see me in my Queen Ann bed, so he would reach as far as his little arms would go and whisper a prayer for me. Telling him that he had "healing hands" planted a seed of faith in him that has carried into his adulthood. His touch and his prayer always left me feeling better.

The more you talk to your children, the more you encourage them to talk. Children are naturally curious. When children are afraid to speak, that curiosity may not be realized.

So what are some of the benefits of good listening comprehension?

- Your child will have a better understanding of what they hear. Remember 45% of communication is hearing.
- They will enjoy a richer vocabulary, which will result in more information about the world around them.
- They will experience better mental imagery of words, resulting in being more creative.
- They will be more expressive in their speech and writing.

Can watching TV improve listening comprehension?

I shared in an earlier chapter how limited TV watching was for our children. It was not because TV watching was a bad thing. Too much of anything can be harmful. I am a Libra, and even though I don't follow my horoscope, I know enough to know that balance is an essential ingredient in how my brain works.

As a parent, I tried to balance our children's engagement in school, extracurricular activities, church, and family time. TV just happened to rank last in terms of importance.

Here are a few advantages that watching TV had on their listening comprehension:

- Hearing and seeing include 2 of 5 senses to help increase their listening comprehension.
- Interesting programs constantly introduced them to new vocabulary words like Quid pro quo from the Lion King.
- Watching TV as a family provided us with opportunities for deep conversations.
- Watching a movie about a book that they have read can increase their listening comprehension. They would look and listen for similarities and differences, as books turned into movies are often not the same.
- Our children could use TV watching to identify and improve content-area knowledge in science, math, geography, history, and even current events.

To make TV watching a more positive experience, these were a few listening comprehension questions that I frequently asked the children.

- Is the family on TV like our family? In what way?
- Do you think that can happen in real life?
- What did you like about the program?
- What would you have done differently?

- Why is this your favorite TV show?

Respond Appropriately: Actually, a response can be appropriate or inappropriate to what was heard. How a child responds depends on how well we concentrate or pay attention, as well as understand or comprehend. Their capacity to do these things will determine their response.

There are several things a parent can do at home to encourage the appropriate response. Most often, children who pay attention and can comprehend will respond favorably. The earlier we emphasize appropriate responses from our children, the better. Innately, children want to please their parents and teachers.

To encourage appropriate responses or behaviors at home and school, start with the following:

- Praise makes children feel good about themselves. Look for opportunities to praise your children or students when they pay attention and show their understanding of what was said or asked.
- The more information they have in advance, the better the chances of success.
- Use a calm tone of voice. Make it your norm.
- Make your requests reasonable. Limit your submissions to 2 or 3 things at a time and be sure they are age-appropriate.

- Make sure that your children have what's needed to carry out the assignment or request.

Observe your child's behavior. If you suspect that there may be an issue behind your child not paying attention or comprehending, seek help. The school is the best place to start as an outside resource. Something as simple as asking your child if he understands can be the insight into a bigger problem.

If you find that your child constantly has problems following simple instructions at home, connect with your child's teacher. Many teachers incorporate mini-lessons on following directions into their lesson plans. In addition, they may be able to suggest some strategies that you can try at home.

Do you feel that you are spending enough time talking to your children? With talking comes the art of listening. Everyone wants to be acknowledged. Good family communication doesn't have to be difficult, but it does take time and patience. Be careful not to talk less with your children as they grow up. Talking and listening become more important as your children grow older.

The best way to raise a good listener is to model being a good listener. It all starts at home. Children who are listened to at home feel loved and have higher self-esteem. They are more willing to share their thoughts and feelings when their voice is being respected and heard.

How do you want to be remembered by your children?

Do you want to be remembered as the mom who always worked and bought them things? Or

the mom who took the time to talk and listen to them? During those talks, you are teaching many life lessons. Your children are opening up about who they are and how they are feeling. This is when you help your children build good character. Teach your children your value system and why it's essential. The school and church can do a lot to instill good character, but ultimately what they value and who they will become will stem from their home environment.

Talking about good character is important, but modeling good character supersedes what we say. Our children will do more of what they see us do than what they hear us say.

When you volunteer your time and resources for a good cause, take your children with you and explain why it's essential to give back and help others.

Be the kind of person that your child wants to emulate. Be approachable so that your children are not afraid to come to you even when they make a mistake. Let your children know that they can make a mistake and still win.

Sometimes getting out of the house will create a neutral environment free of distractions. Our daily walks to the walking trail or in the neighborhood were a special time that provided good listening opportunities for the children and me. Be careful to make this time together with your children a dialogue, not a monologue.

These are special moments that we will cherish for a lifetime. When we finished talking and listening, the sounds of nature replaced the sounds of our voices. We continued to practice our listening in silence.

A wise man will hear and increase in learning, and a man of understanding will acquire wise counsel.
Proverb 1:5 KJV

Adapted by the Author

CHAPTER FOURTEEN

Kids and Peer Pressure: Helpful Guidance for Parents

Outcome

In this chapter, the parent/reader will learn their role in helping their children manage peer pressure.

"Don't be afraid of being different, be afraid of being the same as everyone else.

Author Unknown

"Under pressure, the mouth speaks when the brain is disengaged, and sometimes unwittingly, the gearshift is in reverse when it should be in neutral."

Henry Ford – Founder Ford Motor Company

I define "peer pressure" as being influenced, good or bad, by others.

As a former classroom teacher of elementary and middle school and mother of two, I have witnessed peer pressure more prevalent in middle schoolers than in other grades.

Children seem to care more about what their peers think around the ages of 11-13;

of course, it doesn't start or stop there.

If peer pressure has not arrived at your house, not to worry, it will.

Teachers can be a great resource when it comes to peer pressure. After all, they get to witness your child's engagement with their peers in ways that you don't get to see. As an educator, we are trained to identify the leaders and followers. A good teacher knows the benefit of both and tries to steer each child in the right direction.

The following poem was shared with me several decades ago. I hope it moves you as it did me, which is why I have held on to it all these years later.

Unity

I dreamed I stood in a studio
And watched two sculptors there,
The clay they used was a young child's mind,
And they fashioned it with care.
One was a teacher; the tools he used
Were books and music and art;
One, a parent with a guiding hand
And a gentle, loving heart.
Day after day, the teacher toiled,
With a touch that was deft and sure,
While the parent labored by his side
And polished and smoothed it o'er
And when at last their task was done
They were proud of what they had wrought,
For the things they had molded into the child
Could neither be sold nor bought.
And each agreed he would have failed
If he had worked alone.
For behind the parent stood the school,
And behind the teacher the home.

Anonymous

If you have been an active parent from day one, chances are your children's friends have become accustomed to your presence. This makes peer pressure a bit more manageable for your children, but it still exists. Think of it as a learning experience that all children must go through.

What are some signs that peer pressure has arrived at your house? Maybe your children want to spend more time outside of your home instead of spending family time together. Or perhaps they have become unhappy with their style of clothes. Do they seem to want more name-brand clothes and sneakers?

Any sudden change in the everyday things that never bothered them before may be a sign of peer pressure knocking at your door.

Talking to your children about their new requests can make a huge difference. Don't dismiss their appeal, instead find out why. Not all change is bad. For example, peer pressure can be good or bad. If your children have chosen their friends carefully, there should be little to worry about.

Maybe one of their friends has encouraged them to try a new sport that they have shied away from. If your child's friend introduces your child to his favorite author by sharing books that he has read, that's an example of good peer pressure. On the other hand, if your child's friend encourages your child to drink or smoke or worse, this is the destructive side of peer pressure.

If good values are not instilled in your children, they

will certainly come home to roost. No matter the values, children must find their own way in the world. It will be up to them whether they will accept your value system or not. Their peers will undoubtedly play a part in their journey. Young or old, our peers are a reflection of us. Our children will see themselves in others, and they must decide what is acceptable behavior.

Praise your children for making good choices in friends. Give them lots of affirmations for being themselves and not following the crowd.

There were several instances when our children would come home from school with reports about someone they knew who made a poor choice and faced dire consequences. One instance was when Henry Frank attended the Bridges Classic Football Game, while a group of his friends staged a coup and ended up in court. As parents, we were intentional about how our children spent their free time. They were active members of Bridge Builders of America and Youth United Way from middle school through high school.

When you help your children choose positive extracurricular activities, they are sure to meet a few well-behaved children who share the same values.

Allowing our children to make some of their own decisions helped us know the kind of persons they were becoming. For example, the clothing style that they choose to wear to school, church, and in the community reflects who they are and how they feel about themselves.

We encouraged our children not just to be active in

sports, music, and other organizations, but to lead. We wanted our children to develop as leaders. Their dad and I have always had careers that required strong leadership skills.

I am a firm believer that we should teach our children the things we have learned in life. We knew if they grew up being a leader, they would be less likely to follow the crowd. Instead, the crowd would follow them. We praised our children for taking the lead and for making sound decisions. We emphasized how they were responsible for their actions regardless of the choices their friends made.

We taught them to be compassionate and generous. We can see these things manifested in their adult lives. Mission Accomplished!

"It is not always about winning," I would say. "It is the effort that you put forth that makes the biggest difference."

David Elkind, a child psychologist says, "we often overestimate the influence of a peer group on our children. While the peer group is most influential in matters of taste and preferences, we parents are most influential in more abiding matters of standards, beliefs, and values."

So what can parents do to help their children manage the inevitable pressure from their peers?

Allow your children to make some decisions like:

- What to wear

- What organizations to join
- What sports to play
- What books to read
- What they want for dinner, occasionally

Talk to your children about what friendship means. Put emphasis on what you should not do for your friends.

- I won't cheat or steal for my friends.
- I won't act dumb at school for my friends.
- I won't drink or do drugs for my friends.
- I won't make fun of the less fortunate or handicap for my friends.
- I won't behave irresponsibly for my friends.
- I won't be a bully for my friends.
- I won't disrespect myself or others for my friends.

Remember a big part of parenting is managing ourselves. Consider this as your parenting checklist of things to do often:

- Let your children know when you are proud of their choices
- Teach your children to be independent thinkers
- Encourage your children to develop their special gifts

- Praise your children to enhance their self-esteem
- Regard their feelings and opinions with respect
- Encourage them to excel in something positive
- Stand firm on your family values
- Stress why these values are important
- Urge your children to accept the consequences of their actions
- Respect your children's self-expression and individuality. Let them know that it's OK to be different.
- Enjoy raising the JEWELS that God blessed you with

The more confident our children are within themselves, the less dependent they will be on their peers.

Peer pressure is not always a bad thing. When our children have made good choices in friends, these friends can positively impact our children. It's nice for us to be supportive parents, but children also need supportive friends.

I am blessed to have some of my dearest friends date back to grade school. They know who they are. I added a host of others to this list in junior high, high school, and college.

I have always guarded my friendship space and have tried to teach our children to do the same. There are friends and there are acquaintances. My friendship circle has grown over the years as I have added more strong, courageous, beautiful Christian women along the way through my affiliation with my beloved sorority, Delta Sigma Theta Sorority, Incorporated.

As parents, we must educate ourselves on topics pertaining to our children. The more we learn, the more we can empower our children with skills and tools to lead them to a successful life.

It is our responsibility to help our children make sound decisions because, as Frederick Douglass quotes... "It is easier to raise a child than to rebuild an adult."

Here are a few signs that peer pressure may have arrived at your house:

- Their behavior changes around their friends
- They have started making comparisons to their friends
- They participate in activities that they don't want to do and complain about it
- They express feelings that they don't fit in
- They are focusing more on their image
- Reluctance to go to school

All of the love, time, knowledge, and energy we put into raising our children will be well worth it when they grow up and say,"THANKS" for always being my biggest cheerleader!

Do not be deceived: You cannot do good and keep bad company.

1 Corinthians 15:33 KJV

Adapted by the Author

If you found this parenting book helpful in any way, please leave a review on Amazon. I read every review and they help new readers discover my book.

PRAISE FOR THE AUTHOR

Brenda lives life in step with her purpose. Her first priority is to be the best parent she can possibly be. She raised her children in an atmosphere of loving support and encouragement while instilling in them her Christian values. Her sense of professionalism with strong work ethics and focus on problem-solving gives her the ability to envision possibilities. Brenda maintains personal friendships with her warm smile and infectious personality, which draws you to her.

BEVERLY S. WILLIAMS, PRESIDENT CPR TO LIVE, LLC

From joyous expectancy to birth, Brenda and her husband planned and prayed together for God's grace to cover their children and family. She involved herself in best practices built on foundational Christian promises, including character-building opportunities. God first, then family, has always been her commitment. Brenda was intentional in not only planning legacy family activities but also father-son and mother-daughter outings. Brenda is definitely a role model as a parent!

JAMITA E. SWEARENGEN, CHAIRLADY
MEMPHIS CITY COUNCIL

ABOUT THE AUTHOR

Brenda Reed Pilcher is a proud native Arkansan with a passion for life and laughter. She is the youngest of six siblings who flourished from childhood through college in her beloved hometown of Pine Bluff, Arkansas.

Brenda enjoys traveling with her family and friends, cooking holiday meals, participating in her book club, exercising, conducting parenting seminars, and singing. She also takes pleasure in serving at her church of more than three decades, Mt. Pisgah CME Church, and her sorority of over four decades, Delta Sigma Theta Sorority, Incorporated.

She currently resides in Collierville, Tennessee, with her husband, Henry. They have been happily married for 34 years.

Although teaching was her career choice, Brenda feels that consulting was her destiny. Early in her career, she matriculated from the classroom to make her mark in Educational Instructional Technology (EIT) with an industry leader, Compass Learning, Incorporated. During her 17 years tenure there, Brenda began her life work, empowering parents.

Realizing her gifts, she started an Education

Consulting Service. Her primary focus as President and CEO of her company was to create and deliver customized Professional Development Seminars. These high-level parenting seminars were designed to empower parents, enhance learning, engage families, and build collaboration between the home, school, and community. She later joined Renaissance Learning and retired as a Senior Consultant after 10 years of service.

When asked, how would she like to be remembered? Brenda answered, "PASSIONATE!" Passionate about her faith in God, her family, her friends, and her work.

Her Education

University of Arkansas at Pine Bluff – B.S. Elementary Education and Reading Instruction (K-8)

University of Nebraska at Omaha – M.S. Elementary Education

Numerous company software application certifications

ACKNOWLEDGMENTS

In Memory of:

My dear mother, Willie B. Reed, who was an entrepreneur, who set an example of excellence for me by becoming an educator, seamstress, and cosmetologist simultaneously. I thank her for her dedication to Christ and her family.

My father, Lee Reed, who was also an entrepreneur and a master builder, who taught me to love what I do.

In Honor of:

My sister Diane (Reed) Calhoun, who became our family's matriarch after the passing of our mother, whom she nursed, loved, and cared for. She repeated the same for our father during his illness before his passing. You are the strongest and most giving person I know. Love you, sis!

My Beta Readers: Dr. Betty Johnson, Dr. Noma Anderson, Sandra Verrett, and Carolyn Sanford. Thank you for the honest feedback. It made me a better writer.

My Level-1 Book Launch Team: Valerie Thomas,

Attorney Kelsi J. Pilcher, Valeria Davis, Tunnisha Deer, Crystal Bramlett, Brenda Ingram and Rita Green-Bibbs. Your support in helping me to promote my debut parenting book meant everything!

The Pilcher Family - 2021

Henry & Brenda - 2021